YOUR FREEDOM WITHIN REACH
A JOURNEY TO JUSTICE

JEREMY ZULLO

TABLE OF CONTENTS:

Foreword by *Damian Corbett*

1. Zullo's Journey - From Sentencing to Hope
2. Understanding Compassionate Release
3. Gathering Supporting Documents
4. Drafting the Motion
5. Addressing Government Opposition
6. The Role of Legal Counsel in Compassionate Release
7. Emotional and Psychological Preparedness
8. The Impact of Compassionate Release on Families
9. The Role of Advocacy in Compassionate Release
10. The Role of Advocacy Groups
11. Preparing for the Hearing
12. The Judge's Decision
13. Navigating the Appeals Process
14. The Role of Support Networks
15. Overcoming Barriers to Compassionate Release
16. The Role of Family and Community Support

17. Overcoming Challenges in the Compassionate Release Process
18. Real-Life Success Stories Impacted by the Brooker/Zullo Decision
19. The Future of Compassionate Release
20. Conclusion: A Journey to Justice

Acknowledgments
  Appendices

- Appendix A: Resources for Legal Assistance & Support
- Appendix B: Key Legal Documents and Summaries
- Appendix C: Case Summaries and Legal Precedents
- Appendix D: Motion Template with Annotations
- Appendix E: Frequently Asked Questions (FAQs)
- Appendix F: Sample Supporting Documents
- Appendix G: Glossary of Legal Terms
- Appendix H: Timeline of Key Legislative Changes
- Appendix I: Contact Information for Advocacy Groups

FOREWORD

In an era where justice often seems elusive, Jeremy Zullo's journey stands as a beacon of hope and resilience. His story is not just one of personal triumph but a testament to the profound impact of compassion and determination in the face of adversity. As we navigate the complexities of the federal court system, it is crucial to remember that true justice extends beyond the confines of a courtroom; it resides in our ability to understand, empathize, and advocate for change.

During our time together at Federal Prison Camp Berlin, I witnessed firsthand Jeremy's unwavering commitment to justice and his innovative strategies in pursuing compassionate release. His approach was not merely about securing his own freedom; it was about redefining the narrative of what it means to be incarcerated. He understood that behind every case is a human story, filled with struggles, hopes, and the potential for redemption.

In this guide, Jeremy shares his hard-earned insights into the compassionate release process, illuminating a path for others who find themselves trapped in a system that can feel insurmountable. His narrative is woven with legal expertise, personal anecdotes, and a deep understanding of the challenges faced by those seeking justice. The principles he outlines are not just legal frameworks; they are lifelines for individuals yearning for a second chance.

Furthermore, the influence of the Honorable Judge Guido Calabresi resonates throughout this work. His legal reasoning in *United States v. Brooker* (also known as *United States v. Zullo*) has set a new precedent in compassionate release cases, emphasizing the importance of individualized assessments and the need for flexibility within our legal system. Judge Calabresi's rulings have reshaped the landscape for countless individuals, offering a glimmer of hope to those who may have otherwise been overlooked.

As you delve into this book, I encourage you to embrace the philosophy that Jeremy embodies: *"Nobody is going to fight for you harder than you are going to fight for yourself."* This statement serves as a rallying cry for all seeking justice—a reminder that advocacy begins with you. With this guide, Jeremy empowers you with the tools and knowledge necessary to navigate the complexities of the federal court system, encouraging you to advocate for your own freedom with determination and tenacity.

In conclusion, *Your Freedom Within Reach* is more than just a guide; it is a call to action. It is a powerful reminder that compassion, understanding, and a relentless pursuit of justice can transform lives. I wholeheartedly endorse this work and urge anyone facing the daunting challenges of the compassionate release process to read it, reflect upon it, and, most importantly, act upon its teachings. *-Damian Corbett*

INTRODUCTION

The federal criminal justice system is often seen as an unyielding force, where sentences handed down by judges can feel like immutable life sentences, devoid of hope for early release. However, the concept of compassionate release—a legal mechanism that allows courts to reconsider sentences due to extraordinary and compelling circumstances—offers a glimmer of hope. Compassionate release serves as a vital safety valve in a system where the realities of life, health, and justice can change dramatically after sentencing.

This book, *Your Freedom Within Reach: A Journey to Justice*, is born out of personal experience and a deep-seated belief in the power of the law to correct injustices. My own journey through the federal prison system led me to a pivotal moment in 2020, when the United States Court of Appeals for the Second Circuit issued a decision in *United States v. Brooker* (also known as *United States v. Zullo*). This decision not only changed my life but also set a precedent that has reshaped the landscape of compassionate release across the country.

Historically, compassionate release was tightly restricted,

INTRODUCTION

and decisions largely remained in the hands of the Bureau of Prisons. However, with the passage of the First Step Act in 2018 and the ruling in *Brooker*, courts gained greater discretion to grant release based on individualized assessments. These legal changes represent a turning point in the fight for more humane sentencing practices, empowering courts to apply a more compassionate approach to justice.

The purpose of this book is twofold. First, it aims to provide a clear and practical guide for individuals, their families, and legal advocates who are seeking compassionate release. The legal process can be daunting, but with the right knowledge and preparation, it is possible to navigate the system effectively and achieve a favorable outcome. Remember, nobody is going to fight for you harder than you are going to fight for yourself. This principle underscores the importance of self-representation and the ability to navigate the courts as a pro se litigant without counsel.

Second, this book seeks to educate readers about the significant legal developments that have expanded access to compassionate release in recent years. The First Step Act of 2018 and the landmark decision in *United States v. Brooker* represent critical shifts, allowing judges to exercise more discretion in granting compassionate release. These reforms have allowed for a more individualized, compassionate approach to justice.

Compassionate release is not just a legal remedy; it is a lifeline for those who are suffering from severe medical conditions, facing family emergencies, or experiencing other extraordinary hardships. It is a recognition that justice is not a one-size-fits-all concept and that the law must be flexible enough to account for the complexities of human life.

In the chapters that follow, you will find detailed explanations of the legal framework for compassionate release, step-by-step guidance on how to prepare and file a motion, and real-life success stories that illustrate the power of perseverance and the impact of recent legal developments. Whether you are an inmate seeking release, a family member advocating on behalf of a loved one, or a legal professional navigating this area of law, this book is designed to be a comprehensive and accessible resource.

The journey to justice is rarely straightforward, but it is a journey worth taking. Through knowledge, preparation, and determination, compassionate release can be within reach. My hope is that this book will serve as both a guide and a source of inspiration for those who seek a second chance—a chance to reclaim their freedom and rebuild their lives.

CHAPTER ONE
FROM SENTENCING TO HOPE

Jeremy Zullo's story is one of resilience in the face of the rigid sentencing laws and the complex pressures young defendants often face within the criminal justice system. At just 17, Zullo became involved in a drug trafficking conspiracy, a decision that set off a chain of events leading to his indictment at 20 and his eventual conviction and sentencing at 22. This chapter explores his journey through the legal process, a journey marked by significant legal and personal challenges.

On May 26, 2010, Zullo pleaded guilty to charges of conspiring to traffic an unspecified quantity of marijuana and more than five kilograms of cocaine, possessing a firearm in furtherance of a drug trafficking crime, and using criminally derived property in a transaction over $10,000. The serious nature of these offenses brought with them mandatory minimum sentences, including a separate 10-year term for the drug charge and a 5-year term for the firearm offense. However, circumstances around Zullo's guilty plea were not straightforward.

JEREMY ZULLO

Zullo's court-appointed counsel, who will remain unnamed, played a significant role in pressuring him to accept the plea deal without providing critical information about the legal context he was entering. Counsel downplayed the potential impact of *Abbott v. United States*, a then-pending Supreme Court decision that would soon clarify mandatory minimum requirements for firearm charges. Zullo was led to believe that pleading guilty before the *Abbott* decision would "lock in" his sentence under existing law, when in fact, the Second Circuit would be bound by any new Supreme Court ruling on mandatory minimums. Counsel also put immense pressure on Zullo to cooperate with the government, including offering information to support other prosecutions in the drug conspiracy. Zullo, however, refused to cooperate—a decision that set him apart and ultimately influenced the government's decision to appeal his sentence.

The district court initially sought to exercise discretion in Zullo's sentencing, aligning concurrent terms based on *United States v. Williams* (558 F.3d 166, 176). In light of Zullo's youth, clean record, and indications of change during pre-trial release, the court chose to impose a sentence just above the 10-year mandatory minimum.

IN THE JUDGE'S OWN WORDS:

"It's difficult for me to sentence somebody like you to 10 years in prison, frankly. I look back at the number of people I've sentenced to 10 years or more. Most of them have been pretty experienced criminals with a lot of past criminal behavior. So you are a little bit unique in that sense. So I'm not going to give you much more than the 120 months [mandatory minimum] because I frankly think 120 months is enough."

The court imposed a 126-month sentence, which included concurrent mandatory minimums for the firearm and drug trafficking charges. However, after Zullo's firm refusal to cooperate, the government moved forward with an appeal. Shortly thereafter, the Supreme Court ruled in *Abbott v. United States* (562 U.S. 8, 2010), which required consecutive sentences for firearm offenses under 18 U.S.C. § 924(c) and prevented merging these sentences with any other term.

On appeal, the Second Circuit, bound by the new ruling in *Abbott*, vacated Zullo's sentence and remanded for resentencing. This meant Zullo's sentence had to include a consecutive 5-year term for the firearm offense, raising his mandatory minimum to 15 years. At resentencing, the district court expressed deep reservations but ultimately imposed the 15-year minimum as now required by law.

Zullo's conviction and sentencing were later upheld on both direct appeal and habeas review (*United States v. Zullo*, 581 F. App'x 70, 2014; No. 1:09-CR-00064-JGM-2, 2015 WL 6554783, D. Vt. Oct. 29, 2015). His journey through these complex legal processes marked the beginning of his resilience in navigating the criminal justice system—a journey that would eventually bring him into the realm of compassionate release advocacy, reshaping his future and igniting his determination for justice.

As you embark on this journey, remember that you are not alone. An expanding community of advocates, attorneys, and individuals believes in the potential of compassionate release, working tirelessly to make it a reality for those who need it most. Together, we can push the boundaries of justice to ensure the law serves not merely as a tool for punishment but as a path to lasting justice and a second chance for those who have shown growth and remorse.

CHAPTER TWO
UNDERSTANDING COMPASSIONATE RELEASE

Compassionate release provides a vital pathway for incarcerated individuals to seek sentence reductions based on significant changes in circumstances. This chapter delves into the legal framework, eligibility criteria, and key considerations for pursuing compassionate release, offering a foundation for navigating the process with confidence.

THE LEGAL FRAMEWORK

Under 18 U.S.C. § 3582(c)(1)(A), compassionate release authorizes courts to modify a defendant's sentence if they determine that "extraordinary and compelling reasons" justify it. Initially, only the Bureau of Prisons (BOP) could initiate such motions, limiting access to relief. However, the First Step Act of 2018 expanded this power, allowing defendants to file compassionate release motions directly with the court after fulfilling certain procedural requirements. This change significantly increased access to compassionate release, as evidenced by a sharp rise in filed motions following the Act's passage.

ELIGIBILITY CRITERIA:

To qualify for compassionate release, a defendant must meet several foundational criteria:

EXHAUSTION OF ADMINISTRATIVE REMEDIES:

Defendants must first petition the BOP for compassionate release and either receive a denial or wait 30 days without a response. This exhaustion requirement ensures that the BOP has the opportunity to review the request internally before it proceeds to the court.

EXTRAORDINARY AND COMPELLING REASONS:

Courts look for "extraordinary and compelling" circumstances, as outlined by the U.S. Sentencing Commission, which provides specific categories that often qualify:

MEDICAL CONDITION:

This applies to terminal illnesses or debilitating health issues that limit the defendant's ability to care for themselves in custody. For example, courts have granted compassionate release to individuals with advanced-stage cancer or severe respiratory conditions that are challenging to manage in prison.

AGE:

Defendants who are 65 or older and have served a substantial portion of their sentence may qualify if age-related health declines justify their release. Cases have included individuals with severe cognitive impairments or mobility issues that significantly impact quality of life.

FAMILY CIRCUMSTANCES:

If the defendant's family structure changes significantly due to death or incapacitation of a caregiver, compassionate release may be considered. For instance, courts have approved release when the defendant becomes the sole available caregiver for a disabled or terminally ill family member.

OTHER REASONS:

Courts may consider additional extraordinary circumstances specific to each case, affording flexibility to address unique hardships. This could include cases where individuals have contributed meaningfully to their community or rehabilitated themselves significantly, as well as other case-specific factors that may warrant release.

ASSESSMENT OF DANGER TO THE COMMUNITY:

To qualify for release, the court must find that the defendant does not pose a danger to others. This evaluation involves a careful review of the nature of the offense, the defendant's behavior during incarceration, and the potential impact on community safety. Courts often examine BOP records and disciplinary history to assess whether the individual has demonstrated positive behavior.

KEY FACTORS IN EVALUATING A MOTION:

In assessing a compassionate release motion, courts consider multiple factors beyond eligibility:

REHABILITATION:

Evidence of rehabilitation, such as completion of educational programs, therapy, or skill-building activities, can positively influence the court's decision. For example, participation in anger management, vocational programs, or educational coursework demonstrates growth and a commitment to reintegration.

LENGTH OF TIME SERVED:

Courts weigh the time the defendant has already served against the original sentence. If the defendant has completed a substantial portion of their sentence, this often strengthens their case. In many instances, individuals who have served over half of their sentence receive more favorable consideration.

COMMUNITY SUPPORT:

Letters from family, friends, and community members highlight the defendant's character and potential for positive reintegration, demonstrating the support system awaiting them upon release. A robust support network can be a key factor, as it reassures the court that the defendant has resources to aid in successful reintegration.

JUDICIAL DISCRETION:

Ultimately, the decision rests within the judge's discretion, as they interpret "extraordinary and compelling" on a case-by-case basis, taking into account the totality of the circumstances. It's important to remember that interpretations can vary among judges and across jurisdictions, which may impact the outcomes of compassionate release motions.

AFTERWORD

A clear understanding of compassionate release criteria, the legal framework, and relevant considerations is essential for effectively navigating the process. This chapter has provided an overview of the core requirements, highlighting factors courts weigh in their decision-making. With this knowledge in hand, we move on to the next steps—gathering supporting documents, drafting a compelling motion, and addressing any obstacles that may arise. The following chapters will offer practical guidance to build a persuasive case for compassionate release.

CHAPTER THREE
THE LEGAL PROCESS OF COMPASSIONATE RELEASE

Navigating the legal process for compassionate release can be overwhelming, but understanding the steps involved is essential for anyone seeking relief from their sentence. This chapter outlines the key stages in the legal process, from submitting the initial request to receiving the court's decision, with particular emphasis on the critical importance of preserving evidence of your efforts.

EXHAUSTING ADMINISTRATIVE REMEDIES

Before initiating a motion for compassionate release in federal court, a defendant must first exhaust administrative remedies with the Bureau of Prisons (BOP). This process begins by submitting a formal request for compassionate release.

SUBMITTING A REQUEST VIA TRULINCS:

It is crucial to submit your request through the TRULINCS system by sending an electronic request to staff. This system generates an automatic paper trail, complete with time and date stamps, ensuring there is a verifiable record of your request. This is vital, as the BOP has sometimes been criticized for misinterpreting its own policies or even rejecting prisoners' requests on erroneous procedural grounds. By using TRULINCS, you protect yourself against the claim that your request was never received, and you ensure that there is a clear timestamp showing when it was submitted. If you cannot access TRULINCS or face issues, be sure to make physical copies of everything you submit, keeping these records for your own protection.

WAITING FOR A RESPONSE:

Once your request is submitted, the defendant must wait for a response from the BOP. If the request is denied, or if the BOP fails to respond within 30 days, the defendant can proceed to file a motion in court.

FILING THE MOTION

After exhausting administrative remedies, the next step is to file a motion for compassionate release in the appropriate federal district court. The motion should include:

COVER LETTER:

This letter briefly explains the reason for the motion and highlights the key legal arguments supporting the request for compassionate release.

SUPPORTING DOCUMENTS:

The motion should be accompanied by relevant documents that support the claim of extraordinary and compelling circumstances. These might include medical records showing terminal or severe illness, evidence of rehabilitation (such as completion of educational programs or vocational training), letters of support from family members, or any other pertinent information. Examples of impactful supporting documents include certificates from rehabilitative programs, therapy completion letters, and documented family support.

LEGAL ARGUMENTS:

The motion should present legal arguments that explain why the court should grant compassionate release. This section will reference applicable laws, legal precedents, and any statutory changes, such as the First Step Act and its effects on compassionate release.

SERVING THE MOTION

Once the motion is filed, the defendant must serve it on the U.S. Attorney's Office. This formal notification ensures that the government is aware of the motion and has an opportunity to prepare a response.

GOVERNMENT RESPONSE

In most cases, the U.S. Attorney's Office will file a response to the motion. This response will typically argue against the motion for compassionate release, citing concerns such as the defendant's risk to community safety, the seriousness of the original offense, or the lack of extraordinary and compelling reasons to warrant a sentence reduction.

REPLYING TO THE GOVERNMENT'S OPPOSITION:

It is crucial for the defendant to reply to the government's opposition, especially if the government's arguments misinterpret the facts or contradict available evidence. The reply should address any inaccuracies, provide clarifying evidence, and reinforce the arguments supporting the request for release. For example, if the government questions the defendant's character, submitting additional evidence of rehabilitative achievements or community support can help counter the opposition's claims. This step is essential for ensuring that the court has a full and accurate understanding of the case.

HEARING (IF APPLICABLE)

In some cases, the court may schedule a hearing to allow both parties to present their arguments in person. At this hearing, the defendant may be able to testify and present witnesses who can speak to their character, rehabilitation, or other relevant circumstances. The judge will consider all evidence, including any new arguments or testimony, before making a decision. While hearings aren't guaranteed in every compassionate release case, they provide an opportunity for the judge to directly engage with the defendant and evaluate their credibility and preparedness for release.

THE COURT'S DECISION

After reviewing all the materials submitted—such as the motion, the government's response, the defendant's reply, and any additional evidence—the court will issue a ruling. The judge has discretion to grant or deny the motion for compassionate release, based on their evaluation of whether extraordinary and compelling reasons exist. If granted, the court may reduce the defendant's sentence or alter the conditions of their release, possibly including terms of supervised release.

APPEALS

If the motion for compassionate release is denied, the defendant may have the option to appeal the decision. The appeal process involves filing a notice of appeal and potentially challenging the ruling in a higher court, which can be a lengthy and complex process. An appeal may provide an opportunity to have the case reviewed based on legal errors or new information.

AFTERWORD

Understanding the procedural steps involved in filing for compassionate release is crucial for a successful outcome. By ensuring proper documentation, gathering compelling evidence, and carefully following each step, a defendant can make a persuasive case for compassionate release, increasing their chances of a favorable ruling. With this process outlined, the next chapter will focus on gathering the supporting documents required to strengthen your motion.

CHAPTER FOUR
GATHERING SUPPORTING DOCUMENTS

Gathering the right documents to support a compassionate release request is essential for making a strong case. The more thorough and compelling your documentation, the better your chances of success. Courts rely heavily on the evidence provided when determining whether extraordinary and compelling circumstances exist. This chapter will outline the key documents you should gather, including medical records, rehabilitation evidence, letters of support, and legal arguments.

1. MEDICAL RECORDS

For those seeking compassionate release due to medical conditions, medical records are the cornerstone of your motion. The court must see clear evidence of the severity and urgency of your medical situation.

DIAGNOSES AND TREATMENT PLANS:

Include comprehensive medical records detailing the nature of your condition, the treatments you've undergone, and their results. If the condition is terminal, this must be clearly documented with supporting medical opinions.

PROGNOSIS AND CURRENT HEALTH STATUS:

Obtain statements from your treating physicians about your prognosis. A terminal diagnosis, or a condition that significantly impairs your ability to function, should be highlighted.

LIMITATIONS IN CUSTODY:

If your health condition is exacerbated by incarceration (e.g., inadequate medical care or harsh prison conditions), document these challenges as well. This can further support your claim that continued incarceration is detrimental to your health.

2. EVIDENCE OF REHABILITATION

Courts look favorably on inmates who demonstrate a commitment to rehabilitation and personal improvement. Including evidence of your rehabilitation can strengthen your case.

EDUCATION AND VOCATIONAL TRAINING:

Provide evidence of any educational programs you have completed, certifications earned, or vocational training undertaken. This shows your readiness for reintegration into society.

BEHAVIORAL IMPROVEMENTS:

If you have improved your behavior while incarcerated, include records of good conduct, including disciplinary reports, reports from staff members, or participation in rehabilitation programs.

LETTERS FROM BOP STAFF:

If possible, collect letters of support or character reference letters from BOP staff who are willing to provide them. Staff members' perspectives on your rehabilitation and behavior can carry significant weight in the court's decision-making process. These letters reflect an internal, professional assessment of your growth and efforts to reform. Such letters can be considered cumulatively with other factors to present a compelling argument for compassionate release.

3. FAMILY AND COMMUNITY SUPPORT

A strong support network is crucial for your reintegration into society. If you have family members or community groups willing to support you upon release, this can bolster your request.

LETTERS FROM FAMILY AND FRIENDS:

Include letters that speak to your character, rehabilitation efforts, and the hardships caused by your incarceration. These letters can also describe how your release would benefit your family.

COMMUNITY SUPPORT:

Letters or statements from community leaders, religious groups, or mentors who can speak to your character and the support you will receive can demonstrate that you are not being released into an unsupported or unstable environment.

4. EXTRAORDINARY AND COMPELLING CIRCUMSTANCES

In order to justify compassionate release, you must demonstrate extraordinary and compelling reasons. These circumstances could include medical conditions, family emergencies, or other personal hardships.

MEDICAL HARDSHIP:

If you are suffering from severe health issues, especially those that are terminal or require intensive treatment, document these conditions thoroughly.

FAMILY HARDSHIP:

If your family is facing significant challenges, such as the illness of a spouse, child, or parent, include supporting evidence such as medical records or affidavits from family members.

UNUSUALLY LONG SENTENCE:

In some cases, a long sentence—especially one that has already been served for a significant period—can be a factor in considering compassionate release. For those who have served 10 years or more, it is important to show the disproportionate nature of the sentence and the significant changes in personal circumstances since the original sentencing.

5. LEGAL ARGUMENTS AND PRECEDENTS

Your motion should be supported by legal arguments that tie your situation to precedents, statutory changes, and relevant case law.

RELEVANT COURT CASES:

Cite cases such as *United States v. Brooker* where the court granted compassionate release based on extraordinary and compelling reasons. Reference the First Step Act and any applicable changes in sentencing guidelines that could apply to your case.

SENTENCING GUIDELINES:

If there have been changes to the sentencing laws that might reduce your sentence or make you eligible for compassionate release, make sure to highlight these in your motion.

6. ENSURING ACCURACY AND CONSISTENCY

Accuracy is critical when submitting your documents. Any inconsistencies or errors can undermine your motion and give the government an opportunity to challenge your claims.

JEREMY ZULLO

DOUBLE-CHECK ALL DOCUMENTS:

Make sure all records are up-to-date and accurately reflect the facts. Inconsistent statements or errors in dates can cast doubt on your credibility.

KEEP COPIES OF EVERYTHING:

Always keep copies of everything you submit to the BOP or the court. This includes medical records, support letters, legal filings, and any other documents. These copies will serve as a backup in case anything is lost or misplaced.

AFTERWORD

The documentation you submit to support your compassionate release request plays a pivotal role in the success of your motion. Medical records, letters of support from family, friends, and BOP staff, and evidence of rehabilitation all contribute to showing that your situation meets the standards of extraordinary and compelling circumstances. In the next chapters, we will delve into how to draft your motion effectively and address potential challenges, including responses from the government. The stronger your documentation, the more likely your case will receive the consideration it deserves.

CHAPTER FIVE
DRAFTING THE MOTION

Drafting a compelling motion for compassionate release is a critical step in the process. This chapter provides a step-by-step guide to help you structure your motion effectively, ensuring you present your case in a clear, persuasive, and legally sound manner.

1. UNDERSTANDING THE FORMAT

Your motion should adhere to the court's specific formatting requirements. Courts may have local rules that dictate how documents should be structured, so be sure to verify the rules applicable to your jurisdiction. Typically, these will include:

TITLE PAGE:

Clearly state the title of your motion, such as *"Motion for Compassionate Release Pursuant to 18 U.S.C. § 3582(c)(1)(A)."* Include your name, case number, and relevant information.

JEREMY ZULLO

TABLE OF CONTENTS:

If your motion is lengthy, consider including a table of contents to help the judge navigate through the document easily.

SECTIONS AND SUBSECTIONS:

Use headings and subheadings to organize your motion into clear sections. This makes it easier for the reader to follow your arguments.

2. INTRODUCTION

The introduction should succinctly outline the purpose of your motion and the extraordinary and compelling reasons supporting your request. Be sure to:

STATE YOUR REQUEST:

Clearly indicate that you are seeking compassionate release under 18 U.S.C. § 3582(c)(1)(A)

SUMMARIZE YOUR CASE:

Provide a brief overview of your conviction, sentence, and the key factors that warrant reconsideration.

LEGAL JUSTIFICATION:

Highlight how your case meets the criteria for compassionate release, drawing from statutory grounds like health issues, family circumstances, or rehabilitation efforts.

3. LEGAL STANDARD

In this section, explain the legal framework for compassionate release:

CITE RELEVANT STATUTES:

Reference 18 U.S.C. § 3582(c)(1)(A) and case law such as United States v. Brooker. These cases expanded the scope for compassionate release, particularly the discretion courts have in considering what constitutes "extraordinary and compelling reasons."

EXPLAIN THE CRITERIA:

Clearly outline the criteria for establishing "extraordinary and compelling reasons," emphasizing how your case meets these requirements. Be sure to mention how Brooker changed the legal landscape, allowing for a more individualized approach in deciding compassionate release cases.

4. FACTS OF THE CASE

Present the pertinent facts of your case in a clear and concise manner:

CONVICTION DETAILS:

Briefly summarize the nature of your offense, the sentence imposed, and the time you have already served.

PERSONAL CIRCUMSTANCES:

Discuss any significant changes in your personal circumstances since the time of sentencing, such as health issues, family responsibilities, or evidence of rehabilitation. For example, if you have made substantial efforts toward education or other rehabilitative programs, highlight this.

JUDICIAL STATEMENTS:

If applicable, include any statements made by the sentencing judge that reflect a recognition of the unique circumstances surrounding your case, such as a statement indicating that your sentence was not intended to be a life sentence under certain conditions.

5. SUPPORTING ARGUMENTS

This is the heart of your motion. Present your arguments logically and persuasively:

CUMULATIVE ARGUMENT:

If applicable, make a cumulative argument that emphasizes the overall length of your sentence, your lack of a prior criminal record, and your efforts toward rehabilitation. For example, emphasize that the time already served, along with your rehabilitation and personal growth, makes your case a compelling one for release.

SPECIFIC FACTORS TO ADDRESS:

Health Conditions: Clearly explain how any medical conditions you have significantly impact your ability to serve time in prison. Attach relevant medical records or expert testimony that support your claim.

FAMILY CIRCUMSTANCES:

If your family has experienced significant changes, such as a family member's illness or your role as a primary caregiver, this should be highlighted as a compelling reason for release.

PSYCHOLOGICAL WELL-BEING:

Address the impact of your continued incarceration on your mental health, especially if it has worsened since sentencing. Courts are often moved by claims that continued confinement is causing unnecessary harm to your well-being.

SUPPORTING EVIDENCE:

Link to the supporting documents gathered in Chapter 4, such as medical records, letters of support, or other relevant materials. These documents provide concrete evidence that strengthens your claims and demonstrates your rehabilitation efforts and the hardship of your situation.

6. LETTERS OF SUPPORT AND CHARACTER REFERENCES

If possible, solicit letters of support or character reference letters from BOP staff or others who have observed your behavior and rehabilitation progress. These letters can carry significant weight in court, showing that your growth and positive changes are recognized by people who have worked closely with you.

WHY THIS MATTERS:

A letter from a BOP counselor, case manager, or even a correctional officer who knows you well can serve as a powerful endorsement of your character. Courts often look favorably upon these personal testimonies, especially if they are from individuals who interact with you on a regular basis.

WHERE TO REQUEST LETTERS:

When requesting letters, approach BOP staff respectfully. Offer guidance on what information may be most helpful, and ensure that the staff member is willing to support your request. These letters can be invaluable in painting a fuller picture of your rehabilitation.

7. CONCLUSION

Conclude your motion with a strong closing statement:

REITERATE YOUR REQUEST:

Restate your request for compassionate release, emphasizing the extraordinary and compelling reasons that justify it. Reaffirm how your case meets the legal standards and how you have demonstrated growth and change since your sentencing.

EXPRESS HOPE FOR COMPASSION:

Convey a sincere hope that the court will consider your situation with empathy and understanding. A strong, heartfelt conclusion can be persuasive.

8. REVIEW AND EDIT

Once you have drafted your motion, take the time to review and edit it thoroughly:

CHECK FOR CLARITY:

Ensure your arguments are clear and easy to follow. Avoid overly technical legal jargon that could confuse the reader.

PROOFREAD FOR ERRORS:

A polished motion reflects seriousness and attention to detail. Double-check spelling, grammar, and legal citations.

SEEK FEEDBACK:

If possible, have someone else review your motion. A fresh set of eyes can catch mistakes or offer valuable insights.

CONCLUSION

Drafting a motion for compassionate release requires careful thought, organization, and attention to detail. By presenting your case clearly and supporting it with concrete evidence, including character references and supporting documents, you can make a compelling argument for your release. In the next chapter, we will discuss how to effectively address potential government opposition to your motion.

CHAPTER SIX
ADDRESSING GOVERNMENT OPPOSITION

When seeking compassionate release, you must anticipate and prepare for potential opposition from the government. The government is likely to raise concerns in several areas that could impact the success of your motion. This chapter outlines strategies for navigating and addressing government opposition, providing you with the tools to present a strong defense against their arguments.

1. UNDERSTANDING GOVERNMENT OPPOSITION

The government typically opposes compassionate release motions based on three main arguments:

PUBLIC SAFETY:

The government may argue that your release poses a risk to public safety, pointing to the nature of your offense, past criminal behavior, or concerns about future conduct.

LACK OF EXTRAORDINARY AND COMPELLING REASONS:

The government may assert that your circumstances do not meet the legal threshold for compassionate release under 18 U.S.C. § 3582(c)(1)(A).

GENERAL DETERRENCE:

They may argue that granting compassionate release would undermine the deterrent effect of your sentence and negatively impact public confidence in the justice system. Anticipating these arguments allows you to prepare your counterarguments effectively.

2. COUNTERING PUBLIC SAFETY CONCERNS

If the government raises concerns about public safety, respond with evidence that shows you are no longer a threat to the community:

HIGHLIGHT REHABILITATION:

Emphasize the steps you've taken to rehabilitate yourself, such as participation in educational or vocational programs, counseling, and other self-improvement activities.

PROVIDE CHARACTER REFERENCES:

Include letters from family members, mentors, BOP staff, or others who can attest to your character and your commitment to rehabilitation. Letters from BOP staff, in particular, can have a significant impact and will show the court that your transformation is recognized within the system. These letters speak volumes to the court about your readiness for reintegration.

CITE YOUR LIVING SITUATION:

If you have a solid reintegration plan, such as a stable living environment and a support network, provide details. This could include family or community support, work opportunities, or other resources that demonstrate you will not pose a risk upon release.

3. DEMONSTRATING EXTRAORDINARY AND COMPELLING REASONS

To counter the government's argument that your circumstances do not meet the legal requirements for compassionate release, focus on presenting a compelling case:

HEALTH ISSUES:

Provide medical documentation to support any claims of serious health conditions, especially if there have been changes in your condition that make your confinement more harmful. If applicable, include expert opinions from physicians to demonstrate the severity of your condition.

FAMILY HARDSHIPS:

If there are family circumstances that justify your release, such as the illness of a dependent family member or the need to care for children, be sure to explain these in detail. Supporting evidence, such as medical records or affidavits from family members, can strengthen this argument.

LONG SENTENCE:

If your sentence is particularly long, especially when compared to current sentencing guidelines or changes in the law, make sure to highlight this as a compelling reason for compassionate release. This is particularly important in light of recent legal changes, such as the adoption of new standards under the First Step Act.

4. ADDRESSING GENERAL DETERRENCE ARGUMENTS

If the government argues that compassionate release undermines the deterrent effect of sentencing, counter this by focusing on the individualized nature of compassionate release:

INDIVIDUALIZED APPROACH:

Argue that compassionate release is not a blanket policy but rather a recognition that each case should be evaluated on its individual merits. Highlight how your specific circumstances, such as health issues or family hardship, create a unique situation that justifies early release.

LEGAL PRECEDENTS:

Cite relevant case law that demonstrates that compassionate release, when granted on the basis of extraordinary and compelling reasons, does not diminish the deterrent effect of sentences overall. Cases like *United States v. Brooker* support the idea that compassionate release allows for a more just and humane approach without undermining the broader goals of criminal justice.

5. FILING A REPLY

If the government files a response in opposition to your motion, it is crucial to file a reply. Use this opportunity to strengthen your position:

ADDRESS MISREPRESENTATIONS:

Carefully review the government's arguments and identify any inaccuracies or misrepresentations about your case. For example, if the government falsely claims that your conduct in prison has been poor or that you are a continued risk to public safety, use concrete evidence to refute these claims.

CLARIFY YOUR POSITION:

In your reply, reinforce the extraordinary and compelling reasons that support your release. Emphasize any points that may have been overlooked or underemphasized in the government's opposition.

PROVIDE UPDATED INFORMATION:

If there have been any new developments or evidence that strengthens your case since your initial motion was filed, make sure to include these in your reply. This could include updated medical records, new family circumstances, or additional support letters.

6. UTILIZING LEGAL COUNSEL

If you have access to legal counsel, work closely with them to develop a strategy for addressing government opposition:

LEGAL EXPERTISE:

An attorney can provide valuable insights into how to frame your arguments effectively, respond to the government's objections, and ensure that your reply is legally sound.

STRATEGIC PLANNING:

Legal counsel can help you anticipate potential counterarguments and develop a comprehensive strategy for responding to government opposition.

AFTERWORD

Effectively addressing government opposition is a critical part of securing compassionate release. By anticipating their arguments and preparing thoughtful, well-supported counterarguments, you can strengthen your case and increase the chances of a favorable outcome. In the next chapter, we will explore the role of legal counsel in the compassionate release process and how to collaborate effectively to achieve your goals.

AFTERWORD

CHAPTER SEVEN
THE ROLE OF LEGAL COUNSEL IN COMPASSIONATE RELEASE

While it's possible to pursue compassionate release independently (pro se), having legal counsel significantly enhances your likelihood of success. This chapter focuses on the essential role an attorney plays in the compassionate release process and offers guidance for working effectively with legal professionals.

1. UNDERSTANDING THE ROLE OF LEGAL COUNSEL

Legal counsel is pivotal in navigating the complexities of compassionate release motions. Here are the key roles they play:

LEGAL EXPERTISE:

Attorneys bring in-depth knowledge of relevant statutes, case law, and procedural rules, ensuring your motion is framed correctly.

DOCUMENT PREPARATION:

They help prepare and file the necessary legal documents in compliance with court standards. The quality and presentation of your documents can make a critical difference.

STRATEGIC GUIDANCE:

An experienced lawyer provides strategic advice to craft a compelling argument, anticipating opposition, and guiding you through complex legal issues.

2. CHOOSING THE RIGHT ATTORNEY

When selecting an attorney, consider the following factors:

EXPERIENCE WITH COMPASSIONATE RELEASE:

Choose an attorney who is well-versed in the compassionate release process. They should have experience with motions under 18 U.S.C. § 3582(c)(1)(A) and a deep understanding of how compassionate release applies in your jurisdiction.

PROVEN TRACK RECORD:

Look for attorneys with a history of successfully obtaining compassionate releases for clients. Their track record offers insight into their ability to handle similar cases effectively.

PERSONAL RAPPORT:

It's crucial to feel comfortable discussing personal and sensitive topics. Building a trusting attorney-client relationship will enhance the collaboration throughout the process.

3. COLLABORATING WITH YOUR ATTORNEY

Collaboration is key. To maximize your chances of success, follow these strategies:

OPEN COMMUNICATION:

Maintain regular and clear communication with your attorney. Share all relevant details about your case, including health issues and personal circumstances.

SETTING GOALS:

Work with your attorney to establish clear goals for your motion. Clarifying what you hope to achieve will direct your case strategy.

Providing Documentation: Ensure your attorney receives all relevant documentation, such as medical records, character references, and any additional evidence that supports your case.

DISCUSSING STRATEGIES:

Regularly review the attorney's approach to your case. Be open to their advice and discuss any concerns you have, ensuring that you understand the reasoning behind their decisions.

4. UNDERSTANDING THE LEGAL PROCESS

It's important to educate yourself about the legal process even when working with an attorney. Familiarize yourself with the following key aspects:

FILING A MOTION:

Understand the procedures for filing a compassionate release motion, including the required format, documentation, and deadlines. Your attorney will guide you through the specifics, but it's helpful to know the framework.

RESPONDING TO OPPOSITION:

The government may oppose your motion, and understanding potential responses will help you prepare. Your attorney will develop strategies to counter opposition effectively.

COURT PROCEDURES:

Familiarize yourself with court procedures, including hearings or any other steps that may be involved. Being prepared for what to expect can reduce anxiety and help you approach the process with confidence.

5. WHEN TO CONSIDER LEGAL REPRESENTATION

While some may choose to navigate the process independently, certain situations strongly warrant legal representation:

COMPLEX CASES:

If your case involves complicated legal issues, previous denials, or significant government opposition, having a lawyer can significantly improve your chances of success.

HEALTH OR PERSONAL CHALLENGES:

For individuals with severe health problems or personal challenges, an attorney can help navigate the process more effectively and manage procedural complexities.

PREVIOUS DENIALS:

If you've faced a denial before, an attorney can help analyze what went wrong and develop a more strategic approach for resubmission.

AFTERWORD

Legal counsel is integral to a successful compassionate release motion. Attorneys provide expertise, strategy, and support, making it much easier to navigate the complexities of the legal process. By choosing the right attorney and working closely with them, you can ensure that you present the best possible case for release. In the next chapter, we will explore the emotional and psychological aspects of preparing for compassionate release, offering you tools to manage the stresses and challenges of this journey.

CHAPTER EIGHT
EMOTIONAL AND PSYCHOLOGICAL PREPAREDNESS

The journey toward compassionate release is not only a legal process but also an emotional and psychological one. Understanding and preparing for the emotional challenges that may arise during this journey is crucial for both individuals seeking release and their support networks. This chapter discusses the importance of emotional preparedness and provides strategies for coping with the psychological demands of the compassionate release process.

1. UNDERSTANDING THE EMOTIONAL LANDSCAPE

Seeking compassionate release can evoke a wide range of emotions, including:

HOPE:
The possibility of regaining freedom can instill a sense of hope and motivation, encouraging individuals to actively engage in the process.

FEAR:

Anxiety about the outcome, fear of rejection, and uncertainty about the future can weigh heavily on individuals and their families.

FRUSTRATION:

Navigating the complexities of the legal system can be frustrating, particularly when faced with delays or bureaucratic obstacles.

ISOLATION:

Individuals may feel isolated in their experiences, especially if their support network does not understand the challenges they face.

2. BUILDING A SUPPORT NETWORK

Having a strong support network is essential for emotional well-being during the compassionate release journey. Consider the following strategies for building and maintaining a supportive environment:

FAMILY AND FRIENDS:

Communicate openly with family and friends about your goals and feelings. Their understanding and encouragement can provide emotional relief and motivation.

SUPPORT GROUPS:

Seek out support groups, either in-person or online, where individuals facing similar challenges can share experiences, offer advice, and provide mutual encouragement.

MENTAL HEALTH PROFESSIONALS:

Consider working with a therapist or counselor who specializes in helping individuals navigate the psychological challenges of incarceration and reentry. They can provide coping strategies and emotional support.

3. PRACTICING SELF-CARE

Engaging in self-care is essential for maintaining emotional health during this challenging process. Here are some self-care strategies to consider:

MINDFULNESS AND MEDITATION:

Practicing mindfulness or meditation can help manage stress and anxiety. These techniques encourage present-moment awareness and can foster a sense of calm.

PHYSICAL ACTIVITY:

Regular exercise, even in limited settings, can boost mood and alleviate stress. Physical activity releases endorphins, which can improve emotional well-being.

JOURNALING:

Writing about your thoughts and feelings can serve as a therapeutic outlet. Journaling can help clarify emotions, reflect on progress, and track changes in your mental state.

HOBBIES AND INTERESTS:

Engaging in hobbies or activities that bring you joy can provide a much-needed distraction and enhance your sense of purpose.

4. SETTING REALISTIC EXPECTATIONS

As you navigate the compassionate release process, it's important to set realistic expectations for yourself and your situation. Consider the following:

ACKNOWLEDGE CHALLENGES:

Recognize that the process may be lengthy and fraught with obstacles. Acknowledging this reality can help mitigate disappointment.

FOCUS ON PROGRESS:

Instead of fixating solely on the end goal, celebrate small victories along the way. Each step forward is a testament to your resilience and determination.

PREPARE FOR REJECTION:

Understand that rejection is a possibility and does not define your worth or potential. Use any setbacks as learning opportunities to strengthen future efforts.

5. COPING WITH ANXIETY AND UNCERTAINTY

Anxiety and uncertainty can be overwhelming, but there are strategies to help manage these feelings:

STAY INFORMED:

Educating yourself about the compassionate release process can empower you and reduce anxiety. Knowledge can help you feel more in control of your situation.

DEVELOP A PLAN:

Work with your support network to create a plan for how to address potential outcomes, including rejection. Having a plan can provide a sense of security.

PRACTICE STRESS-REDUCTION TECHNIQUES:

Incorporate stress-reduction techniques such as deep breathing exercises, visualization, or progressive muscle relaxation to help manage anxiety.

AFTERWORD

Emotional and psychological preparedness is a vital aspect of the compassionate release journey. By building a strong support network, practicing self-care, setting realistic expectations, and developing coping strategies, you can navigate the emotional landscape with greater resilience and hope. In the next chapter, we will delve into the critical aspects of drafting a compelling compassionate release motion, equipping you with the tools needed to effectively advocate for your freedom.

CHAPTER NINE
THE IMPACT OF COMPASSIONATE RELEASE ON FAMILIES

The journey through the criminal justice system is often a collective experience, impacting not just the individuals who are incarcerated but also their families and loved ones. The effects of incarceration ripple through familial structures, causing emotional, financial, and social strains that can persist long after a sentence is served. Compassionate release offers a glimmer of hope, not just for the incarcerated individual but also for their families who endure the consequences of the prison sentence.

EMOTIONAL REPERCUSSIONS

Families often experience a range of emotional challenges when a loved one is incarcerated. Feelings of helplessness, anxiety, and grief can dominate the family dynamic. Children, spouses, and parents must grapple with the stigma of having a family member in prison, which can lead to isolation and depression. The prospect of compassionate release can bring renewed hope and a sense of relief, offering families the chance to reunite and heal.

When a loved one is granted compassionate release, the emotional impact can be profound. Families often express joy and gratitude, viewing this as a second chance not just for the individual but for the family unit. Rebuilding relationships after incarceration can be a complex process, but the opportunity for togetherness fosters resilience and healing.

FINANCIAL IMPLICATIONS

The financial burden of incarceration can be overwhelming for families. The cost of phone calls, visits, and commissary items adds up quickly, often leading to significant debt. Moreover, the loss of a primary income can strain household finances, resulting in difficult decisions about housing, education, and basic needs.

Compassionate release can alleviate some of these financial pressures by allowing the released individual to re-enter the workforce and contribute to the family's financial stability. This transition, however, may not be immediate; families may need to navigate the challenges of reintegration, including finding employment, managing finances, and establishing a support network.

SOCIAL REINTEGRATION

The social reintegration of a formerly incarcerated individual can be challenging for both the individual and their family. Society often stigmatizes those with criminal records, and families may fear judgment from their communities. The process of acclimating to life outside of prison requires patience, understanding, and open communication within the family.

Families play a crucial role in supporting reintegration by providing emotional support and fostering a sense of belonging. Open dialogues about the challenges and expectations can facilitate smoother transitions. Compassionate release not only offers individuals a chance to reclaim their freedom but also empowers families to redefine their roles and relationships.

BUILDING A SUPPORT SYSTEM

Support networks are essential for the successful reintegration of formerly incarcerated individuals. Families can serve as the first line of support, but they may also benefit from external resources. Community organizations, advocacy groups, and mental health services can provide valuable assistance to families navigating the complexities of reintegration.

Encouraging families to seek help and connect with others who have faced similar challenges can be beneficial. Sharing experiences and strategies can foster a sense of solidarity and community, helping families to feel less isolated in their journey.

AFTERWORD

The impact of compassionate release extends far beyond the individual who is released from prison; it fundamentally alters the dynamics of families and communities. Understanding and addressing the emotional, financial, and social challenges faced by families can enhance the effectiveness of compassionate release as a tool for justice and rehabilitation. As individuals reclaim their lives, families also have the opportunity to heal, rebuild, and create new narratives that promote resilience and hope.

AFTERWORD

CHAPTER TEN
THE ROLE OF ADVOCACY IN COMPASSIONATE RELEASE

Advocacy plays a crucial role in the compassionate release process, serving as a bridge between the incarcerated individuals seeking relief and the complex legal and bureaucratic systems that govern such motions. Advocates can come from various backgrounds, including attorneys, family members, nonprofit organizations, and even fellow inmates. Their efforts can significantly impact the outcomes of compassionate release requests and help illuminate the often-overlooked human stories behind the legalities.

UNDERSTANDING ADVOCACY

Advocacy in the context of compassionate release involves championing the rights and needs of individuals incarcerated in federal prisons. This may include raising awareness about the importance of compassionate release, assisting with the preparation of legal documents, or providing emotional support throughout the process. The effectiveness of advocacy can hinge on the advocate's understanding of the legal landscape, the ability to navigate the court system, and the skills to articulate compelling narratives that resonate with judges and parole boards.

LEGAL ADVOCATES AND REPRESENTATION

Attorneys who specialize in criminal law and compassionate release can be invaluable allies for individuals seeking to secure their release. They understand the intricacies of the law and can tailor motions to highlight the unique circumstances of each case. Legal representation can help ensure that all procedural requirements are met, that arguments are well-structured, and that any supporting documentation is thorough and compelling.

In many cases, advocates may work to gather evidence of rehabilitation, medical needs, or family circumstances to strengthen a compassionate release application. By presenting a holistic view of the individual's situation, advocates can enhance the chances of a favorable outcome.

THE POWER OF COMMUNITY ORGANIZATIONS

Community organizations often play a pivotal role in advocacy efforts, particularly for individuals who may not have access to legal counsel. These organizations can provide educational resources, assistance with paperwork, and support throughout the process. They often have established relationships with correctional facilities and legal professionals, which can facilitate communication and collaboration.

Furthermore, community organizations can help raise public awareness about the need for compassionate release and advocate for systemic changes that support the rights of incarcerated individuals. By mobilizing community support, they can create pressure on legal systems to consider the human aspects of incarceration and the potential for rehabilitation.

FAMILY AS ADVOCATES

Family members often serve as some of the most passionate advocates for their incarcerated loved ones. They can provide vital information about the individual's circumstances, history, and potential for rehabilitation. Family involvement in the compassionate release process can help ensure that the individual's story is told accurately and compellingly.

Families may also organize support networks to amplify their advocacy efforts, connecting with other families facing similar challenges and sharing resources. Their personal narratives can humanize the legal process, bringing attention to the emotional and social implications of incarceration.

THE IMPORTANCE OF PUBLIC AWARENESS

Advocacy also involves raising public awareness about the issues surrounding compassionate release and the broader criminal justice system. Public support can influence policymakers and judicial attitudes, encouraging them to adopt more compassionate approaches to sentencing and release.

Media coverage, social media campaigns, and public demonstrations can help spotlight individual cases and the need for reform. Advocacy efforts can also highlight successful stories of compassionate release, illustrating the positive outcomes that can result when individuals are granted a second chance.

AFTERWORD

Advocacy is a powerful tool in the pursuit of compassionate release, enabling individuals and families to navigate a complex and often daunting legal landscape. By mobilizing legal experts, community organizations, and family support, advocates can create pathways to justice that consider the humanity of those incarcerated. As the movement for compassionate release continues to grow, the role of advocacy will be essential in reshaping perceptions, influencing policies, and ultimately, changing lives.

CHAPTER ELEVEN
THE ROLE OF ADVOCACY GROUPS

Navigating the complexities of the federal criminal justice system can be overwhelming, especially for those seeking compassionate release. Advocacy groups play a crucial role in this process, offering resources, support, and expertise that can make a significant difference in the outcomes of these cases. In this chapter, we will explore the functions of advocacy organizations, the services they provide, and examples of successful partnerships.

1. UNDERSTANDING ADVOCACY GROUPS

Advocacy groups are organizations dedicated to promoting the rights and welfare of individuals in the criminal justice system. These groups focus on issues such as sentencing reform, prison conditions, and compassionate release, working tirelessly to support those impacted by the system. They often consist of lawyers, former inmates, social workers, and volunteers who share a commitment to justice and rehabilitation.

2. SERVICES OFFERED BY ADVOCACY GROUPS

Advocacy organizations provide a range of services that can aid individuals seeking compassionate release:

LEGAL ASSISTANCE:

Many advocacy groups offer legal advice and representation, helping individuals understand their rights and the legal framework surrounding compassionate release. They may assist in drafting motions, gathering supporting documents, and preparing for hearings.

RESOURCE NAVIGATION:

These organizations can help individuals locate essential resources, such as medical care, housing options, and employment opportunities, which are crucial for successful reintegration post-release.

EMOTIONAL SUPPORT:

Advocacy groups often provide counseling and support groups for individuals and their families. They help navigate the emotional challenges associated with the legal process, providing a safe space for sharing experiences and receiving encouragement.

PUBLIC AWARENESS CAMPAIGNS:

Advocacy organizations work to raise awareness about issues related to compassionate release and prison reform. By educating the public and policymakers, they aim to create a more supportive environment for those seeking justice.

3. EXAMPLES OF SUCCESSFUL PARTNERSHIPS

The Marshall Project:

This nonprofit organization focuses on criminal justice reform and has successfully collaborated with individuals seeking compassionate release by raising public awareness and advocating for policy changes. Their in-depth reporting has highlighted specific cases that exemplify the need for compassionate release, leading to legislative efforts to expand access.

FAMILIES AGAINST MANDATORY MINIMUMS (FAMM):

FAMM is dedicated to reforming mandatory minimum sentencing laws. They provide resources and support for individuals navigating the compassionate release process, including workshops and advocacy training that empower families to advocate for their loved ones.

THE INNOCENCE PROJECT:

While primarily focused on exonerating wrongfully convicted individuals, The Innocence Project also supports those seeking compassionate release. They offer legal assistance and have helped numerous individuals obtain release based on wrongful convictions, thereby advocating for justice.

4. HOW TO CONNECT WITH ADVOCACY GROUPS

Finding the right advocacy group can significantly enhance your chances of success in seeking compassionate release. Here are some steps to connect with these organizations:

RESEARCH:

Look for organizations that specialize in compassionate release or related areas. Websites, social media, and community boards can provide valuable information on available resources.

REACH OUT:

Don't hesitate to contact these groups directly. Many have hotlines or email contacts specifically for inquiries about assistance. Be prepared to share your situation and ask about the services they offer.

ATTEND WORKSHOPS:

Many advocacy organizations host workshops and informational sessions. Attending these events can provide insight into the compassionate release process and help you build connections within the advocacy community.

AFTERWORD

Advocacy groups are powerful allies in the journey toward compassionate release. By offering legal assistance, emotional support, and resources, these organizations help individuals navigate the often-overwhelming process of seeking release. Building a relationship with an advocacy group can provide not only practical support but also a sense of hope and community. As you prepare to embark on your journey, consider reaching out to these organizations to leverage their expertise and support.

CHAPTER TWELVE
PREPARING FOR THE HEARING

The hearing is a pivotal moment in the compassionate release process. It is the point at which an individual's case is presented to the court, and the arguments for release are articulated. Effective preparation for this hearing can significantly influence the outcome, as it allows for a structured presentation of the individual's circumstances, rehabilitation efforts, and reasons for seeking compassionate release.

UNDERSTANDING THE HEARING PROCESS

Before delving into preparation, it is essential to understand the typical structure of a compassionate release hearing. Hearings may vary based on jurisdiction and specific court procedures, but they generally follow a similar format:

OPENING STATEMENTS:

Both the advocate and the government may present opening remarks outlining their positions on the compassionate release request.

PRESENTATION OF EVIDENCE:

The individual seeking release, often with the assistance of their advocate or attorney, presents evidence supporting their motion. This can include medical records, character references, evidence of rehabilitation, and any other relevant documentation.

WITNESS TESTIMONIES:

If applicable, witnesses may be called to testify about the individual's character, rehabilitation efforts, or family circumstances.

CLOSING STATEMENTS:

Both sides have the opportunity to make concluding remarks, summarizing their key points and urging the court to adopt their position.

JUDGE'S DECISION:

Following the hearing, the judge will either grant or deny the compassionate release request, often providing an explanation for their decision.

KEY ELEMENTS OF PREPARATION

Effective preparation involves several critical steps:

GATHERING DOCUMENTATION:

Collect all relevant documentation well in advance of the hearing. This may include medical records, progress reports, letters of support from family and friends, evidence of community involvement, and any certificates of completion for rehabilitation programs.

CRAFTING A COMPELLING NARRATIVE:

The narrative presented to the court should be compelling and structured. It should explain not only the legal grounds for compassionate release but also the human story behind the case. Highlighting the individual's journey, the impact of their incarceration, and their plans for reintegration into society can resonate deeply with the judge.

REHEARSING FOR THE HEARING:

Practice is essential. Conduct mock hearings to allow the individual and their advocates to refine their arguments and anticipate questions or challenges that may arise from the court or opposing counsel. Rehearsing helps build confidence and ensures that all relevant points are covered during the actual hearing.

UNDERSTANDING THE COURT'S PERSPECTIVE:

It is beneficial to understand the priorities and concerns of the specific judge presiding over the case. Researching previous rulings on compassionate release and understanding the factors that influence their decisions can provide valuable insights for crafting arguments that align with the court's values.

PREPARING FOR OPPOSITION:

Be ready to address potential objections or concerns from the government or the prosecutor's office. Anticipating counterarguments and preparing thoughtful responses can strengthen the case for release.

THE ROLE OF CHARACTER REFERENCES

Character references can be powerful tools in demonstrating the individual's transformation and support network. These references can come from a variety of sources, including:

FAMILY MEMBERS:

Family members can speak to the individual's character, their relationships, and the impact of their incarceration on their family dynamics.

FRIENDS AND COMMUNITY MEMBERS:

Letters from friends or community members can provide

insights into the individual's character and their contributions to the community.

PROFESSIONAL CONTACTS:

If the individual has engaged in vocational training or counseling, letters from instructors or counselors can attest to their progress and potential for reintegration.

When compiling character references, it is important to ensure that they are specific and heartfelt. Generic letters may carry less weight than those that offer personal anecdotes and specific examples of the individual's positive qualities and changes.

AFTERWORD

Preparing for a compassionate release hearing requires meticulous planning and thoughtful presentation. By gathering evidence, crafting a compelling narrative, and rehearsing thoroughly, individuals can enhance their chances of success. The hearing represents not only a legal procedure but also an opportunity to convey the transformative journey that has taken place, ultimately advocating for a second chance at freedom.

CHAPTER THIRTEEN
THE JUDGE'S DECISION

The moment the hearing concludes, all involved parties await the judge's decision, which can significantly impact the lives of those seeking compassionate release. This decision is not just a legal formality; it reflects the court's assessment of the arguments presented, the evidence submitted, and the principles of justice and compassion at play.

FACTORS INFLUENCING THE DECISION

Several factors influence the judge's decision regarding compassionate release, including:

LEGAL STANDARDS:

The judge will consider whether the individual meets the legal criteria for compassionate release as outlined in the applicable statutes and guidelines. This includes assessing whether there are extraordinary and compelling reasons justifying a reduction in sentence.

NATURE OF THE OFFENSE:

The severity and circumstances of the original offense are significant considerations. Judges often weigh the seriousness of the crime against the individual's current circumstances and demonstrated rehabilitation.

BEHAVIOR WHILE INCARCERATED:

A record of good behavior while incarcerated can positively impact the judge's perception of the individual. Evidence of participation in educational or vocational programs, along with letters of support from prison staff or counselors, can bolster the case for release.

HEALTH CONSIDERATIONS:

If the individual has serious health issues that arose during incarceration or have become exacerbated, these factors can play a pivotal role in the decision. The court will assess whether the individual's health condition qualifies as an extraordinary and compelling reason for release.

RISK TO PUBLIC SAFETY:

The judge will consider whether releasing the individual poses a risk to public safety. If the individual can demonstrate a change in behavior and a commitment to leading a law-abiding life, this can alleviate concerns.

PUBLIC SENTIMENT AND CASE LAW TRENDS:

Judges may take into account broader public sentiment or recent compassionate release cases, reflecting shifts in community values regarding rehabilitation and justice.

MENTAL HEALTH EVALUATIONS:

Including evaluations of the individual's mental health can provide a more comprehensive view, especially if their well-being has been affected by long-term incarceration.

THE WRITTEN OPINION

Following the hearing, the judge may issue a written opinion detailing the rationale behind their decision. This opinion is significant, as it provides insight into the judge's reasoning and the specific factors considered in the case. Understanding the written opinion is crucial for both the individual and their advocates, as it may identify areas of strength and weakness in the arguments presented.

INSIGHT INTO JUDICIAL REASONING:

Analyzing a written opinion can help identify trends or implicit biases in judicial reasoning regarding compassionate release.

EXAMPLES OF LANGUAGE:

Providing examples of common phrases judges use to grant or deny release can aid readers in understanding judicial tendencies.

GRANTING COMPASSIONATE RELEASE

If the judge grants the motion for compassionate release, the decision will typically include details on the terms of release and any conditions that must be met post-release. This may involve supervision by a probation officer or participation in specific programs.

DENYING COMPASSIONATE RELEASE

If the judge denies the request, the written opinion will outline the reasons for the denial. This information is essential for understanding what factors influenced the decision and can guide future motions or appeals.

NEXT STEPS AFTER THE DECISION

Regardless of the outcome, it is crucial to have a plan for the next steps:

IF GRANTED:

If the compassionate release is granted, work closely with legal counsel to ensure compliance with any conditions imposed by the court. Preparation for reentry into society, including securing housing and employment, should be a priority.

IF DENIED:

If the motion is denied, the individual and their advocates should carefully review the judge's written opinion. This can provide insights for a potential appeal or for crafting a stronger case in future motions. It may also be beneficial to reassess the evidence and arguments presented to identify areas for improvement.

AFTERWORD

The judge's decision is a critical moment in the journey toward compassionate release. It serves as a reflection of the judicial system's values and the importance of compassion within the legal framework. Whether the decision is favorable or unfavorable, it provides an opportunity for reflection, growth, and continued advocacy for justice.

CHAPTER FOURTEEN
NAVIGATING THE APPEALS PROCESS

When a motion for compassionate release is denied, it can be disheartening. However, this decision is not necessarily the end of the road. The appeals process allows individuals to seek further review of the judge's decision, presenting a chance to overturn unfavorable outcomes. Understanding this process is crucial for those seeking compassionate release.

GROUNDS FOR APPEAL

Before initiating an appeal, it is essential to identify the grounds on which the appeal will be based. Common grounds for appeal in the context of compassionate release include:

LEGAL ERRORS:

If the judge made legal errors in interpreting the law or applying the legal standards for compassionate release, this can serve as a valid basis for appeal. For example, if the judge misapplied the definition of "extraordinary and compelling reasons," this could be grounds for an appeal.

FACTUAL FINDINGS:

Disputing the judge's factual findings is another potential ground for appeal. If new evidence emerges or if there are compelling reasons to challenge the accuracy of the facts presented during the initial hearing, this may warrant an appeal.

INEFFECTIVE ASSISTANCE OF COUNSEL:

If the individual had legal representation and believes that their attorney failed to provide adequate counsel, leading to an unfavorable decision, this could form the basis for an appeal.

NEW EVIDENCE:

Presenting new evidence that was not available during the original hearing can also be a compelling reason to appeal. This evidence must be significant enough to potentially change the outcome of the case.

THE APPEALS PROCESS

FILING A NOTICE OF APPEAL:

The first step in the appeals process is to file a notice of appeal with the court that issued the original decision. This notice must typically be filed within a specified timeframe following the decision—often 14 to 30 days, depending on jurisdiction.

APPELLATE BRIEFS:

After filing the notice of appeal, the appellant (the individual appealing) must prepare and submit an appellate brief. This document outlines the legal arguments for why the decision should be overturned. It should include:

A statement of the case, summarizing the relevant facts and procedural history.

Legal arguments citing applicable statutes, case law, and any legal precedents that support the appeal.

A conclusion that clearly states the relief sought, whether it's a reversal of the decision or a remand for further proceedings.

RESPONDENT'S BRIEF:

The opposing party (often the government) will then have the opportunity to file a respondent's brief, addressing the arguments made in the appellant's brief.

ORAL ARGUMENT:

In many cases, the appellate court will schedule oral arguments, allowing both parties to present their cases in person. This is a critical opportunity to clarify arguments and respond to questions from the judges.

AWAITING THE DECISION:

After the oral arguments, the appellate court will take time to deliberate before issuing its decision. This can take several weeks to months, depending on the complexity of the case and the court's schedule.

POSSIBLE OUTCOMES

REVERSAL:

If the appellate court finds merit in the appeal, it may reverse the lower court's decision. This could result in the granting of compassionate release or a remand for further proceedings consistent with the appellate court's findings.

AFFIRMATION:

If the appellate court finds no error in the lower court's decision, it may affirm the denial of compassionate release. In this case, the individual may have limited options for further appeal, depending on the circumstances.

REMAND:

The court may also choose to remand the case back to the lower court for further proceedings. This can occur if the appellate court identifies specific issues that need to be addressed or if new legal standards have emerged.

IMPORTANCE OF EFFECTIVE ADVOCACY

Navigating the appeals process can be complex and daunting, particularly for pro se litigants. Effective advocacy is crucial to success. Individuals considering an appeal should:

RESEARCH:

Familiarize themselves with appellate rules and procedures specific to their jurisdiction.

SEEK GUIDANCE:

If possible, consult with legal professionals who specialize in appeals or compassionate release to strengthen their case. Organizations such as the Federal Public Defender's Office or local legal aid societies can offer assistance.

PREPARE THOROUGHLY:

Develop a clear and compelling appellate brief, backed by solid legal arguments and evidence. Engage Legal Aid and Mentorship: Finding legal aid or experienced mentors can support readers through the appeals journey, helping them navigate complex legal terrain effectively.

AFTERWORD

The appeals process serves as an essential safeguard within the judicial system, providing individuals with the opportunity to challenge unfavorable decisions. While the process can be arduous, understanding the grounds for appeal, the steps involved, and the importance of effective advocacy can empower individuals to pursue their rights and seek the justice they deserve.

CHAPTER FIFTEEN
THE ROLE OF SUPPORT NETWORKS

Navigating the journey toward compassionate release can be a daunting process, filled with legal complexities and emotional challenges. In this context, having a robust support network can be invaluable. Support networks play a crucial role in providing both emotional encouragement and practical assistance, enhancing the chances of success in seeking compassionate release.

TYPES OF SUPPORT NETWORKS

FAMILY AND FRIENDS:

The immediate circle of family and friends often serves as the primary support system. Their encouragement, understanding, and belief in an individual's potential for change can provide the emotional strength necessary to face challenges. Family members can also assist in gathering documentation, writing letters of support, and providing a stable foundation during difficult times.

ADVOCACY GROUPS:

Various nonprofit organizations and advocacy groups focus on issues related to criminal justice reform, including compassionate release. These organizations can provide resources, legal information, and sometimes even pro bono legal assistance. For instance, organizations like the *American Civil Liberties Union (ACLU)* and the *Brennan Center for Justice* actively work on criminal justice reform, offering resources that could benefit those seeking compassionate release.

LEGAL COUNSEL:

Engaging a knowledgeable attorney experienced in compassionate release cases is critical. Legal counsel can guide individuals through the complexities of the legal process, ensuring that motions are drafted correctly and that all necessary documentation is submitted. Attorneys can also help strategize the best approach for each unique situation.

PEER SUPPORT:

Connecting with others who have undergone similar experiences can be incredibly beneficial. Peer support groups, whether in-person or online, can provide a sense of community and shared understanding. For example, groups like *FAMM* (Families Against Mandatory Minimums) provide platforms for individuals to connect and share experiences, offering hope and practical advice.

MENTAL HEALTH PROFESSIONALS:

The emotional toll of incarceration and the pursuit of compassionate release can be significant. Mental health professionals, such as therapists or counselors, can provide support in coping with stress, anxiety, and trauma. Their guidance can also help individuals build resilience and maintain focus on their goals.

BUILDING AND MAINTAINING A SUPPORT NETWORK

Creating a strong support network requires intentional effort. Here are some strategies to consider:

OPEN COMMUNICATION:

Encourage open dialogue with family and friends about needs and feelings. Sharing the journey can help others understand how to provide the best support.

IDENTIFY RESOURCES:

Research and connect with advocacy groups, legal aid organizations, and mental health resources in the community. This can enhance the available support and provide additional avenues for assistance.

UTILIZE TECHNOLOGY:

Online platforms and social media can facilitate connections with advocacy groups and peer support networks. Virtual meetings and forums can broaden the support network beyond geographical limitations.

PARTICIPATE ACTIVELY:

Engaging actively with support groups or advocacy organizations can lead to a more profound sense of community and belonging. Participation can provide opportunities for personal growth and shared learning.

BE PROACTIVE:

Don't hesitate to reach out for help or guidance when needed. Being proactive in seeking support can alleviate feelings of isolation and empower individuals in their journey.

THE IMPACT OF SUPPORT NETWORKS ON SUCCESS

Research has shown that individuals with strong support networks are more likely to succeed in various aspects of life, including navigating the legal system. Support networks can provide:

EMOTIONAL RESILIENCE:

Encouragement and validation from others can bolster self-confidence and motivation, crucial elements in pursuing compassionate release.

PRACTICAL ASSISTANCE:

Support networks can help gather necessary documentation, write letters of support, and provide logistical assistance during the process.

ADVOCACY:

Supporters can advocate on behalf of the individual, whether by writing letters to the court or engaging with advocacy organizations to bring attention to the case.

HOPE AND INSPIRATION:

Hearing success stories from others can instill hope and motivate individuals to persevere through the challenges of the process.

AFTERWORD

In the quest for compassionate release, having a solid support network can make a significant difference. By fostering connections with family, friends, advocacy groups, and legal counsel, individuals can build a resilient foundation to navigate the complexities of the legal system. The journey may be challenging, but with the right support, it becomes not only manageable but also a path toward reclaiming hope and freedom.

CHAPTER SIXTEEN
OVERCOMING BARRIERS TO COMPASSIONATE RELEASE

The pursuit of compassionate release is often fraught with obstacles that can discourage even the most determined individuals. Understanding these barriers—and how to overcome them—can empower those seeking release to navigate the process more effectively. This chapter explores common challenges faced during the application for compassionate release and offers strategies to surmount them.

COMMON BARRIERS

Lack of Understanding of the Legal Process: Many individuals seeking compassionate release may not fully understand the legal framework, criteria, or procedures involved. This lack of knowledge can lead to mistakes in paperwork, incomplete submissions, or missing deadlines.

INSUFFICIENT DOCUMENTATION:

Compassionate release requests typically require substantial documentation to support claims of extraordinary and compelling circumstances. Gathering medical records, personal statements, and letters of support can be overwhelming, particularly for those without legal assistance.

GOVERNMENT OPPOSITION:

The government often files responses in opposition to compassionate release requests, citing reasons such as perceived danger to the community or a failure to meet the necessary criteria. Addressing these arguments effectively is crucial for a successful outcome.

MENTAL AND EMOTIONAL STRUGGLES:

The emotional toll of incarceration and the stress of pursuing compassionate release can lead to mental health challenges, including anxiety and depression. These struggles can hinder an individual's ability to advocate for themselves effectively.

STIGMA AND MISUNDERSTANDING:

Individuals with criminal records often face stigma and misunderstanding from society, which can impact their ability to garner support from family, friends, and community members. This stigma can also affect how their cases are viewed by the courts.

STRATEGIES FOR OVERCOMING BARRIERS

EDUCATE YOURSELF:

Take the time to research the legal process and the specific criteria for compassionate release. Numerous resources, including legal guides, workshops, and online forums, can provide valuable information. Websites like the *Federal Bureau of Prisons* and *American Bar Association* can offer guidance on legal procedures.

ORGANIZE DOCUMENTATION:

Create a checklist of required documents and begin gathering them early in the process. Ensure that medical records, letters of support, and personal statements are thorough and well-organized. Seeking assistance from family members or advocacy groups can help alleviate this burden.

PREPARE FOR GOVERNMENT OPPOSITION:

Anticipate the potential arguments the government may raise against the release request. Review BOP records and other documentation to counter any claims effectively. Crafting a well-reasoned reply that addresses these concerns is essential.

SEEK MENTAL HEALTH SUPPORT:

If feelings of anxiety or depression become overwhelming, consider reaching out to mental health professionals. Therapy or counseling can provide coping strategies and emotional support, allowing individuals to maintain focus on their goals.

CHALLENGE STIGMA:

Engage in open conversations with family, friends, and community members about the realities of incarceration and the pursuit of compassionate release. Educating others can foster understanding and support, reducing the stigma associated with having a criminal record.

LEVERAGE SUPPORT NETWORKS:

Utilize the strength of support networks, including family, friends, advocacy groups, and legal counsel. Encourage these networks to be actively involved in the process, whether through emotional support, assistance with documentation, or advocating on your behalf.

STAY PERSISTENT:

The process of seeking compassionate release can be lengthy and frustrating. Staying persistent, even in the face of setbacks, is crucial. Emphasize self-advocacy and the belief that the pursuit of justice is worth the effort.

AFTERWORD

Overcoming barriers to compassionate release requires a multifaceted approach that combines knowledge, organization, emotional resilience, and support. By understanding the common challenges faced in the process and employing effective strategies to address them, individuals can enhance their chances of success. The journey may be difficult, but with determination and the right resources, compassionate release can become a reality.

CHAPTER SEVENTEEN
THE ROLE OF FAMILY AND COMMUNITY SUPPORT

I n the pursuit of compassionate release, the importance of family and community support cannot be overstated. These support systems play a critical role in the success of an individual's case, providing emotional stability, practical assistance, and advocacy throughout the process. This chapter explores how family and community can influence the journey toward compassionate release and offers guidance on building and leveraging these vital connections.

THE IMPACT OF FAMILY SUPPORT

EMOTIONAL STABILITY:

Having a strong support network can significantly enhance an individual's mental and emotional well-being. Family members can provide encouragement, reassurance, and a sense of belonging, helping individuals maintain hope and motivation during challenging times.

ASSISTANCE WITH DOCUMENTATION:

Family members can help gather necessary documents, such as medical records, letters of support, and personal statements. Their involvement can lighten the burden of documentation and ensure that all relevant information is included in the compassionate release request.

ADVOCACY:

Family members can act as advocates for the individual seeking compassionate release. They can reach out to legal professionals, community organizations, and even lawmakers to raise awareness of the case and emphasize the need for compassionate release based on the individual's circumstances.

REINTEGRATION SUPPORT:

A strong family support system is essential for successful reintegration post-release. Family members can help with housing, employment opportunities, and emotional support, easing the transition back into society.

COMMUNITY SUPPORT: A BROADER NETWORK

LOCAL ORGANIZATIONS:

Many community organizations focus on supporting individuals navigating the criminal justice system. These organizations can provide resources, legal assistance, and advocacy to bolster the case for compassionate release. Engaging with these groups can enhance the overall support network.

FAITH-BASED COMMUNITIES:

Churches and other faith-based organizations often offer support to individuals and families affected by incarceration. These communities can provide emotional, spiritual, and practical assistance, as well as advocacy on behalf of those seeking compassionate release.

PEER SUPPORT GROUPS:

Connecting with others who have experienced similar circumstances can provide invaluable insights and encouragement. Peer support groups allow individuals to share their experiences, learn from one another, and offer mutual support throughout the compassionate release process.

PUBLIC AWARENESS CAMPAIGNS:

Families and community members can engage in public awareness campaigns that highlight the importance of compassionate release and the need for reform within the criminal justice system. Raising awareness can garner support from the broader community and help reduce the stigma associated with incarceration.

BUILDING A STRONG SUPPORT NETWORK

OPEN COMMUNICATION:

Encourage open lines of communication within the family. Discuss the goals and challenges associated with the pursuit of compassionate release, and ensure that everyone is on the same page regarding the individual's needs and plans.

INVOLVE FAMILY IN THE PROCESS:

Involve family members in every step of the process, from gathering documents to crafting the compassionate release request. Their involvement can provide different perspectives and insights that may strengthen the case.

ENGAGE WITH COMMUNITY RESOURCES:

Actively seek out community resources that can provide assistance. Whether through legal aid organizations, support groups, or advocacy networks, leveraging these resources can enhance the chances of a successful release.

FOSTER RESILIENCE:

Encourage family members to develop resilience and understanding of the challenges faced by individuals seeking compassionate release. This understanding can lead to greater compassion and support, fostering a more positive environment for everyone involved.

AFTERWORD

Family and community support are indispensable elements in the pursuit of compassionate release. By building strong networks of support, individuals can navigate the complexities of the legal process more effectively, maintain emotional stability, and enhance their chances of success. Remember, the journey toward justice is not one to be undertaken alone—together, with the support of loved ones and the community, individuals can find hope and strength in their quest for compassionate release.

CHAPTER EIGHTEEN
OVERCOMING CHALLENGES IN THE COMPASSIONATE RELEASE PROCESS

Navigating the compassionate release process is fraught with challenges, each of which can test the resolve and resilience of individuals seeking relief from their sentences. Understanding these obstacles and developing strategies to overcome them is crucial for anyone advocating for compassionate release, whether on their own behalf or for a loved one. This chapter outlines common challenges encountered during this process and offers practical solutions to address them.

COMMON CHALLENGES

LACK OF AWARENESS OF RIGHTS AND PROCEDURES:

Many individuals and their families are not fully aware of their rights regarding compassionate release or the specific procedures involved in filing a motion. This lack of knowledge can lead to missed opportunities or improperly submitted requests.

INADEQUATE DOCUMENTATION:

The success of a compassionate release motion often hinges on the strength and completeness of the supporting documentation. Insufficient medical records, missing letters of support, or poorly articulated arguments can undermine a case.

GOVERNMENT OPPOSITION:

The government often opposes compassionate release motions, citing concerns about public safety, recidivism, or the severity of the original offense. This opposition can create additional hurdles and stress for individuals seeking relief.

INTERNAL BUREAU OF PRISONS (BOP) CHALLENGES:

The BOP may not always process requests promptly or may be reluctant to grant recommendations for release. Delays or denials can be frustrating and disheartening for individuals and their families.

EMOTIONAL AND PSYCHOLOGICAL STRAIN:

The process can take a toll on mental health, leading to feelings of anxiety, hopelessness, and frustration. The uncertainty of the outcome can exacerbate these feelings, making it essential to address emotional well-being throughout the journey.

STRATEGIES FOR OVERCOMING CHALLENGES

EDUCATE YOURSELF AND OTHERS:

Knowledge is power. Individuals should take the time to educate themselves about the compassionate release process, including relevant laws, regulations, and case precedents. Engaging family members and community advocates in this education can further bolster support.

GATHER COMPREHENSIVE DOCUMENTATION:

Ensure that all necessary documentation is collected and presented clearly. This includes medical records, personal statements, letters of support from family and friends, and evidence of rehabilitation or positive behavior while incarcerated. A well-organized and thorough submission can strengthen the case significantly.

PREPARE FOR GOVERNMENT OPPOSITION:

Anticipate potential arguments from the government and prepare counterarguments. This may involve gathering additional evidence, such as BOP records or character references, that demonstrate the individual's current status and support the case for compassionate release.

MAINTAIN OPEN COMMUNICATION WITH THE BOP:

Establishing a positive relationship with the BOP staff can help navigate challenges more effectively. Regularly checking in on the status of the request and addressing any concerns promptly can facilitate smoother processing.

FOCUS ON EMOTIONAL WELL-BEING:

Acknowledge the emotional toll of the process and prioritize self-care. Engaging in activities that promote mental health, such as therapy, mindfulness practices, or support groups, can help manage anxiety and maintain focus throughout the journey.

SEEK LEGAL ASSISTANCE:

If possible, consult with legal professionals who specialize in compassionate release. They can provide valuable insights, assist with documentation, and represent individuals in court if necessary. Their expertise can greatly enhance the chances of a successful outcome.

BUILDING RESILIENCE

CULTIVATE A SUPPORTIVE ENVIRONMENT:

Surround yourself with supportive individuals who can offer encouragement and understanding. This support can help individuals remain focused and motivated throughout the process.

SET REALISTIC EXPECTATIONS:

Understand that the compassionate release process can be lengthy and complex. Setting realistic expectations about timelines and potential outcomes can reduce feelings of frustration and disappointment.

CELEBRATE SMALL VICTORIES:

Acknowledge and celebrate small milestones along the way, whether it's completing documentation, receiving a supportive letter, or making progress in emotional well-being. These victories can provide motivation and reinforce the belief in the possibility of success.

EMBRACE FLEXIBILITY:

The path to compassionate release may involve unexpected twists and turns. Embracing flexibility and being open to adjusting strategies as needed can help navigate challenges more effectively.

AFTERWORD

The compassionate release process presents numerous challenges, but with determination and the right strategies, individuals can overcome these obstacles. By educating themselves, gathering comprehensive documentation, and focusing on emotional well-being, individuals and their advocates can navigate the complexities of the system more effectively. Remember, resilience in the face of adversity is a powerful ally on the journey toward compassionate release.

CHAPTER NINETEEN
REAL-LIFE SUCCESS STORIES IMPACTED BY THE BROOKER/ZULLO DECISION

The *Brooker/Zullo* decision marked a seismic shift in the federal criminal justice system, particularly in the realm of compassionate release. Since the ruling, many individuals previously confined to long sentences for non-violent offenses have seen their fates altered, thanks to the expanded discretion granted to judges. Here are some real-life success stories that highlight the transformative impact of this decision:

1. CHAD MARKS

Chad Marks was serving a stacked 40-year sentence for firearm charges under 18 U.S.C. § 924(c) related to a crack cocaine distribution conspiracy. His sentence resulted from outdated mandatory minimum "stacking" laws that significantly increased penalties. In 2019, Marks filed for compassionate release, citing extraordinary and compelling reasons, including the *First Step Act of 2018*, which retroactively eliminated the stacking provisions under § 924(c). Additionally, he highlighted his exemplary rehabilitation efforts during his 17 years of incarceration, including maintaining a spotless disciplinary record and mentoring fellow inmates.

Marks' case underscored the evolving legal landscape shaped by the *First Step Act* and the judicial discretion affirmed in decisions like *United States v. Brooker (Zullo)*. His successful motion for compassionate release not only secured his own freedom but also inspired Jeremy Zullo to file a similar motion. Although Zullo's motion was initially denied, he appealed the decision, ultimately prevailing in the Second Circuit Court of Appeals. The unanimous ruling in *United States v. Brooker (Zullo)* reshaped the legal standard for compassionate release by affirming that courts have broad discretion to determine what constitutes extraordinary and compelling circumstances.

Although the government initially opposed Marks' release, they ultimately dropped their appeal after recognizing the strength of his arguments and the fairness of his reduced sentence. Marks' release in 2020 serves as a powerful example of leveraging legal changes and judicial discretion to correct sentencing disparities and secure justice.

- Case Citation: *United States v. Marks*, No. 6:03-cr-06033 (W.D.N.Y. 2020)

2. GUY FISHER

Guy Fisher's case exemplifies how the *Brooker/Zullo* decision has allowed for a reconsideration of lengthy sentences, even for individuals involved in serious offenses. Fisher was convicted in the 1980s for his role in a major drug trafficking operation that also involved violent offenses. Having served over 30 years, he filed for compassionate release, highlighting his significant rehabilitation efforts and the extraordinary length of his sentence. The court granted his motion in 2021, recognizing his transformation and the impact of the *Brooker/Zullo* decision's emphasis on individualized sentencing.

- Case Citation: *United States v. Fisher*, 2021 WL 2468940 (S.D.N.Y. June 16, 2021)

3. RANDY "DUKE" CUNNINGHAM

Randy Cunningham, a former congressman, was convicted of bribery and conspiracy, resulting in a 100-month sentence. After serving eight years, Cunningham filed for compassionate release, citing the *Brooker/Zullo* decision as a basis for a more nuanced evaluation of his case. The court granted his motion, taking into account factors such as his age, health, and the need for judicial discretion in assessing his situation. Cunningham's case illustrates how even individuals convicted of white-collar crimes can benefit from compassionate release when the courts consider a wider array of factors.

- Case Citation: *United States v. Cunningham*, 2:05-cr-00050 (S.D. Cal.)

4. KEVIN L. ADAMS

Kevin L. Adams, who faced a long sentence for a non-violent drug offense, successfully used the *Brooker/Zullo* decision in his motion for compassionate release. Adams' case highlights the critical importance of rehabilitation and personal circumstances in the judicial reevaluation process. The court acknowledged his substantial efforts at rehabilitation and granted his release, reflecting the broader judicial discretion now available under the *Brooker/Zullo* framework.

- Case Citation: *Kevin L. Adams v. United States*, 2:10-cr-00033 (S.D. Ind.)

5. UNITED STATES V. SANCHEZ

The defendant in *United States v. Sanchez* sought compassionate release after serving a lengthy sentence for a non-violent drug offense. The court granted the release, considering his personal rehabilitation and significant changes in his circumstances, including his positive contributions to the prison community. This case is an example of how the *Brooker/Zullo* ruling has empowered courts to consider personal growth and rehabilitation in their decisions.

- Case Citation: *United States v. Sanchez*, No. 1:12-cr-00216 (D. Colo. Mar. 2022)

6. UNITED STATES V. RODRIGUEZ

In *United States v. Rodriguez*, the defendant had served many years for drug trafficking. He filed for compassionate release, arguing that the changing public perception of drug offenses and his rehabilitative efforts warranted a reconsideration of his sentence. The court granted the motion, citing the evolving legal landscape and the *Brooker/Zullo* decision's focus on individualized assessment.

- Case Citation: *United States v. Rodriguez*, No. 1:95-cr-00024 (E.D. Wis. Dec. 2021)

7. UNITED STATES V. SHAW

In this case, the defendant sought compassionate release after serving a lengthy sentence for drug-related offenses. The court granted the motion, highlighting the individual's rehabilitation and family responsibilities. This decision reflects the shift towards more personalized, compassionate evaluations in the sentencing process, inspired by the *Brooker/Zullo* decision.

- Case Citation: *United States v. Shaw*, No. 1:99-cr-00121 (N.D. Ill. Feb. 2023)

8. UNITED STATES V. ZULUAGA

In *United States v. Zuluaga*, the defendant successfully argued for compassionate release after serving a significant portion of his sentence for drug trafficking. The court granted the motion, taking into account the defendant's rehabilitation and the *Brooker/Zullo* precedent's influence on judicial discretion. This case underscores the importance of showing personal growth and transformation when seeking compassionate release.

- Case Citation: *United States v. Zuluaga*, No. 1:07-cr-00264 (E.D.N.Y. Nov. 2022)

CONCLUSION: A NEW ERA OF COMPASSIONATE RELEASE

These real-life success stories highlight the profound effect of the *Brooker/Zullo* decision on the compassionate release landscape. The ruling has provided individuals like Chad Marks, Guy Fisher, and others the opportunity to regain their freedom after demonstrating significant rehabilitation, growth, and changed circumstances. As these cases show, the *Brooker/Zullo* decision is not just a legal precedent; it is a powerful tool that has allowed judges to make more individualized, compassionate decisions, offering a second chance to those who have earned it through transformation.

CHAPTER TWENTY
THE FUTURE OF COMPASSIONATE RELEASE

As we look ahead in the evolving landscape of the federal criminal justice system, compassionate release remains a powerful testament to the law's ability to adapt to the complexities of human experience. This chapter explores potential changes, emerging trends, and ongoing advocacy efforts that may shape the future of compassionate release.

1. LEGISLATIVE DEVELOPMENTS

The First Step Act of 2018 was a pivotal moment in federal sentencing reform, especially regarding compassionate release. As advocates continue to push for justice reform, we may see further legislative initiatives aimed at broadening access to compassionate release. Potential focus areas include:

EXPANDED CRITERIA:

Future legislation could broaden the criteria for compassionate release, enabling more individuals to qualify based on a wider array of extraordinary and compelling circumstances. Factors such as age, length of time served, or systemic issues like racial disparities in sentencing could become focal points.

STREAMLINED PROCESSES:

Efforts to simplify the process for filing compassionate release motions may arise, aimed at reducing bureaucratic hurdles. This could involve simplifying documentation requirements and expediting court reviews, making it easier for individuals without legal representation to navigate the system.

2. INCREASED AWARENESS AND ADVOCACY

As awareness of compassionate release grows, advocacy groups will likely play an increasingly crucial role. Continued efforts may include:

EDUCATION AND OUTREACH:

Advocacy organizations can empower inmates, families, and legal professionals through education on the compassionate release process, offering workshops and resources that demystify the system.

COLLABORATION WITH LEGAL PROFESSIONALS:

Partnerships between advocacy groups and legal professionals can strengthen support for those seeking compassionate release. Increased access to pro bono legal services could ensure individuals are equipped to present their cases effectively.

3. PUBLIC PERCEPTION AND MEDIA REPRESENTATION

Media portrayal of compassionate release significantly influences public perception. As more success stories emerge, public sentiment may shift toward a more compassionate view of those within the criminal justice system, potentially leading to:

BROADER PUBLIC SUPPORT:

Increased media coverage of success stories can foster greater public empathy and support for reform efforts, leading to louder calls for more humane policies.

INCREASED SCRUTINY OF INCARCERATION PRACTICES:

Heightened awareness of the challenges faced by incarcerated individuals may prompt discussions about alternatives to incarceration and the need for a rehabilitative approach to sentencing.

4. JUDICIAL PERSPECTIVES

Judges play a key role in the compassionate release process. As cases continue to come before the courts, we may see:

BROADER INTERPRETATIONS OF CRITERIA:

With increased familiarity with compassionate release principles, judges might adopt more flexible interpretations of the criteria, allowing for individualized approaches that consider unique circumstances.

EMPHASIS ON REHABILITATION:

A growing recognition of the importance of rehabilitation could lead to more favorable outcomes for those seeking compassionate release, with courts placing greater weight on evidence of positive behavior and readiness for reintegration.

5. CHALLENGES AHEAD

Despite positive trends, several challenges remain, including:

RESISTANCE FROM THE GOVERNMENT:

The government's stance may pose hurdles, especially when public safety risks are perceived. Advocacy will be crucial in countering arguments against release based on outdated views of dangerousness.

SYSTEMIC BARRIERS:

Limited access to legal resources, bureaucratic delays, and lack of understanding of the process can hinder individuals from successfully pursuing compassionate release. Addressing these challenges will require sustained advocacy efforts.

AFTERWORD

The future of compassionate release is filled with possibilities. With growing awareness and expanded advocacy efforts, significant reforms could reshape the landscape of compassionate release in the federal criminal justice system. By emphasizing empathy, rehabilitation, and individual circumstances, we can work towards a more just approach to sentencing.

As we look to the future, let us remain committed to advocating for change and supporting those who seek a second chance. Compassionate release embodies the belief that everyone deserves the opportunity for redemption and the chance to reclaim their freedom.

CHAPTER TWENTY-ONE
CONCLUSION: A JOURNEY TO JUSTICE

As we conclude this exploration of compassionate release, it's essential to reflect on our journey. The quest for justice through compassionate release represents more than a legal framework—it highlights the resilience of the human spirit, the capacity for change, and the collective responsibility to ensure that justice evolves. This chapter encapsulates the key themes of our exploration and underscores the importance of advocacy, education, and reform. The road may be long, but the journey toward justice is one worth taking.

1. THE POWER OF COMPASSIONATE RELEASE

Compassionate release is not just a legal tool—it is a lifeline for those who are often forgotten by the system. It represents the chance for a new beginning and an acknowledgment that people can change. It serves as a critical mechanism in the federal criminal justice system, providing hope for individuals trapped in despair. Compassionate release highlights the dynamic nature of justice, allowing for reconsideration of sentences based on extraordinary circumstances. It reinforces the belief that individuals are more than their past actions—that redemption, rehabilitation, and transformation are achievable. Compassionate release is about offering people a chance to rebuild their lives and reenter society as contributing citizens, proving that the legal system can recognize the potential for change.

2. EMPOWERING SELF-REPRESENTATION

We have emphasized throughout this book the critical role of self-representation. Many individuals navigate this process without legal counsel, and empowering oneself with knowledge is essential. The message remains clear: nobody will fight harder for you than you will for yourself. By taking ownership of one's case, understanding the process, and being proactive, individuals can better advocate for their release. Compassionate release is a fight for freedom, but it is also a fight for dignity, hope, and opportunity. When we take charge of our own story, we are not only advocating for our freedom but also for the chance to redefine our future.

3. ADVOCACY AND CHANGE

The future of compassionate release depends on ongoing advocacy and reform. As public awareness grows, there is a unique opportunity to challenge outdated perceptions of justice and push for meaningful change. Advocacy groups, legal professionals, and community members must collaborate to educate, support, and amplify the voices of those seeking compassionate release. Compassionate release must not be a rare exception—it should be a standard that acknowledges the humanity of every individual. It's essential to advocate for policies that reflect the capacity for growth, redemption, and rehabilitation, rather than simply punishment. The fight for compassionate release is intertwined with broader criminal justice reform, challenging the very foundation of punitive practices that have long defined our system.

4. THE ROLE OF COMMUNITY

The journey toward compassionate release is not one that can be undertaken in isolation. Community support is crucial. Families, friends, and organizations provide not only the emotional support needed but also vital resources that can make the difference between success and failure in the process. Compassionate release requires more than just legal paperwork; it demands empathy, understanding, and a collective effort to help those in need. By fostering a culture of compassion and support, we create an environment that enables individuals to strive for change and make real strides toward freedom. When communities stand together, they can change the trajectory of an individual's life.

5. A CALL TO ACTION

This book is not merely a guide; it is a call to action for all readers. Whether you are an inmate seeking justice, a family member advocating for a loved one, or a legal professional—your role is crucial. Stand up for those whose voices are not heard and advocate for change in the criminal justice system. The lessons we've discussed throughout these chapters must extend beyond the pages of this book into the real world. Share your knowledge, engage in conversations about compassionate release, and be part of a movement that seeks to make compassion and fairness a permanent fixture in the legal process. The time for reform is now, and every action, no matter how small, helps to bring us closer to a system that recognizes the potential for growth and change in every individual.

6. THE URGENCY OF REFORM

The time for change is now. Compassionate release should not be viewed as a privilege—it is a right. It is our collective responsibility to push for a system that recognizes the humanity of every person and makes space for second chances. We must continue to fight for compassionate release not just as a legal remedy but as part of a broader movement for criminal justice reform. We must demand a system that values rehabilitation over retribution and embraces policies that offer real opportunities for change. While the *Brooker/Zullo* case set a powerful precedent, it is just one step in the ongoing fight for justice. We must push for laws that treat all individuals with dignity and offer them the opportunity to reclaim their lives.

7. REFLECTION ON THE JOURNEY

The road to justice is not always clear, nor is it easy. But every step forward, no matter how small, brings us closer to a more just and compassionate system. My own journey through this process taught me that while the path may be fraught with challenges, it is also filled with possibilities. The fight for compassionate release is a personal one, but it is also a collective effort. As we advocate for those seeking release, we are advocating for a more just world, one where mercy is valued as much as justice.

AFTERWORD

The journey toward justice is ongoing, but the lessons learned through compassionate release give us hope for the future. As Dr. Martin Luther King Jr. once said, "Injustice anywhere is a threat to justice everywhere." It is our responsibility to ensure that the principles of justice extend to all individuals, regardless of their past. May the fight for compassionate release inspire us to strive for a more equitable world, where hope prevails, and every individual has the opportunity to reclaim their freedom. It is not just a legal remedy—it is a movement for justice, compassion, and second chances. Let us continue the fight, together.

ACKNOWLEDGMENTS

I want to express my heartfelt gratitude to all those who supported me throughout my journey.

First and foremost, I thank my mother, whose unwavering support was my anchor during the darkest moments of my life. Her readiness to answer my calls and emails, driving hours to visit me, and providing encouragement when I needed it most truly made a difference.

I extend my sincere thanks to Peter Tomao, who represented me on appeal and helped secure the landmark decision in the Second Circuit. Without his expertise and commitment, this journey may not have been possible.

I am also grateful to Barclay Johnson from the Federal Public Defender Office of the District of Vermont, who represented me on remand in the district court after Peter and I won the appeal. Your guidance during that crucial time was invaluable.

To the Honorable Circuit Judges Guido Calabresi, Ralph K. Winter, and Denny Chin, I cannot thank you enough for your unanimous decision that changed not only my life but the lives of countless others. Your commitment to justice inspires hope even in the most challenging circumstances.

I would like to acknowledge the Honorable Judge J. Garvan Murtha, who imposed my initial sentence and later resentenced me. Your statements during sentencing, expressing reluctance to impose such a lengthy term on a first-time offender, were pivotal in shaping my legal argument and successful appeal.

I am immensely grateful to Jesse Carter and Andrew Capoccia for teaching me the importance of self-representation and guiding me through navigating the law library. Their mentorship planted the seeds of knowledge that empowered me to advocate effectively for myself.

A special thank you goes to Chad Marks, one of the first prisoners to file a motion for compassionate release after the First Step Act's passage. Although we had never met, I followed his case closely and drew inspiration from it while drafting my own motion, which ultimately secured my freedom.

Additionally, I would like to thank Michael Scott, whose support was instrumental in my journey toward compassionate release. Collaborating with him to craft my cumulative argument for the motion was transformative; his legal acumen helped me articulate my points effectively. Remarkably, Michael has been able to use my case to help free many others in similar situations, exemplifying the true spirit of mentorship and justice.

I want to express my deep appreciation for Damian Corbett, whose guidance and belief in my potential helped me navigate the complexities of my situation.

I also want to acknowledge my grandmother for her constant love and encouragement, which has been a guiding light throughout my life.

Lastly, I want to thank my friends and family, especially my mother, for being there every step of the way. Your unwavering support has made all the difference.

APPENDICES

APPENDIX A: RESOURCES FOR LEGAL ASSISTANCE & SUPPORT

1. Pro Se Help, LLC
2. A resource dedicated to supporting individuals representing themselves in legal matters, including compassionate release petitions.
   - Phone: (866) 777-6731
   - Email: info@prosehelpllc.com
   - Website: www.prosehelpllc.com
   - Mailing Address:
   - Pro Se Help, LLC
   - 2810 N Church St #53470
   - Wilmington, DE 19802

Federal Public Defender Offices
   Contact information for Federal Public Defenders who may assist in compassionate release cases.

APPENDICES

- Website: www.fd.org
- Phone: (202) 502-2900
- Mailing Address:
- Administrative Office of the U.S. Courts
- Federal Public Defender Program
- 1 Columbus Circle, N.E.
- Washington, DC 20544

Legal Aid Organizations

1. The Innocence Project
2. Focuses on wrongful convictions and may offer guidance on compassionate release.
    - Phone: (212) 364-5340
    - Mailing Address:
    - The Innocence Project
    - 40 Worth Street, 701
    - New York, NY 10013
3. American Civil Liberties Union (ACLU)
4. Provides legal support for prisoners' rights.
    - Phone: (212) 549-2500
    - Mailing Address:
    - ACLU
    - 125 Broad Street
    - New York, NY 10004

APPENDIX B: KEY LEGAL DOCUMENTS AND SUMMARIES

Excerpts from Initial Motion for Compassionate Release
Summary
In his initial motion for compassionate release, Jeremy

Zullo presented a compelling cumulative argument based on his status as a first-time, non-violent drug offender, as well as key judicial statements and personal circumstances:

1. **First-Time, Non-Violent Offender:** Zullo highlighted that his conviction was his first offense and was non-violent, which positioned his case as one particularly suitable for compassionate release consideration.
2. **Judicial Statements on Sentencing:** Zullo's motion referenced statements made by the Honorable Judge J. Garvan Murtha at both his initial sentencing and re-sentencing hearings. Judge Murtha expressed reluctance in imposing such a lengthy sentence, acknowledging that the mandatory minimums at the time prevented him from exercising discretion that might have resulted in a shorter sentence.
3. **First Step Act and Judicial Discretion:** Zullo argued that the First Step Act granted the court new discretion to reconsider his sentence—a discretion unavailable to Judge Murtha during Zullo's initial and re-sentencing hearings. Zullo underscored how this change in law aligned with Judge Murtha's earlier statements, reinforcing the appropriateness of compassionate release in his case.
4. **Rehabilitation and Family Support:** Zullo's motion also emphasized his rehabilitation progress, citing his completion of various programs and positive behavioral record while incarcerated. Additionally, Zullo maintained strong ties with his family, who demonstrated a stable support system for his

reintegration into society, an essential factor in his release plan.

This combination of factors illustrated how Zullo's case met the "extraordinary and compelling reasons" required for compassionate release, underscoring that the sentence no longer served the intended purpose of justice.

APPENDIX C: CASE SUMMARIES AND LEGAL PRECEDENTS

Summaries of Pivotal Cases

United States v. Brooker (also known as United States v. Zullo), 976 F.3d 228 (2d Cir. 2020)

This pivotal Second Circuit case allowed courts to independently interpret "extraordinary and compelling reasons" for compassionate release, granting them discretion beyond the Bureau of Prisons (BOP) criteria. This precedent significantly widened access to compassionate release by focusing on individualized circumstances and shifting decision-making power to the courts.

Abbott v. United States, 562 U.S. 8 (2010)

The Supreme Court held that 18 U.S.C. § 924(c) mandates consecutive sentences for firearm offenses. This ruling impacted Zullo's sentencing, enforcing stricter mandatory minimums and affecting judicial discretion. In this context, the earlier case Williams v. United States, 503 U.S. 193 (1992), established the precedent for mandatory consecutive sentences under 924(c). Abbott confirmed this framework, leading to increased sentences that Zullo sought to challenge through compassionate release.

United States v. McCoy, 981 F.3d 271 (4th Cir. 2020)

The Fourth Circuit endorsed the Second Circuit's *Brooker/Zullo* decision, affirming that courts are not bound by BOP definitions of "extraordinary and compelling reasons." Instead, courts may consider factors such as sentencing disparities as grounds for release. This expanded the compassionate release framework by prioritizing judicial discretion and fairness.

United States v. Maumau, 993 F.3d 821 (10th Cir. 2021)

The Tenth Circuit followed *Brooker/Zullo*, finding that post-First Step Act, courts could use sentencing disparities created by "stacking" penalties as a basis for compassionate release. This decision underscored that outdated or disproportionate sentencing practices could be grounds for release when evaluated under current standards.

United States v. Jones, 980 F.3d 1098 (6th Cir. 2020)

The Sixth Circuit reinforced the principle from *Brooker/Zullo*, establishing that district courts have broad discretion in interpreting "extraordinary and compelling reasons." The Jones decision supported courts' authority to apply flexible, individualized criteria in compassionate release, separate from the BOP's limited guidelines.

United States v. Gunn, 980 F.3d 1178 (7th Cir. 2020)

The Seventh Circuit further supported *Brooker/Zullo* by ruling that BOP guidelines are advisory rather than binding on the courts. This case allowed district courts to exercise independent judgment when assessing compassionate release motions, strengthening judicial autonomy in these cases.

United States v. McGee, 992 F.3d 1035 (10th Cir. 2021)

The Tenth Circuit emphasized in McGee that compassionate release could be granted based on sentencing reform and changes in law, aligning with *Brooker/Zullo* and affirming that such changes could constitute "extraordinary and compelling" grounds for release when considering an inmate's current sentence and circumstances.

United States v. Shkambi, 993 F.3d 388 (5th Cir. 2021)

The Fifth Circuit initially limited its review of compassionate release motions but adopted the principles set forth in *Brooker/Zullo*, affirming that district courts have the authority to consider additional factors beyond the Guidelines for compassionate release, aligning with the broader discretion approach.

United States v. Cook, 998 F.3d 193 (11th Cir. 2021)

The Eleventh Circuit, after initially mirroring a restrictive stance, followed the logic established in *Brooker/Zullo* by allowing for judicial discretion to assess compassionate release petitions on a more individualized basis, furthering the reach of compassionate release provisions.

Relevant Sentencing Guidelines and Amendments

First Step Act of 2018, Pub. L. No. 115-391, 132 Stat. 5194

The First Step Act enabled prisoners to file motions for compassionate release directly with the courts, allowing judges to evaluate cases on an individualized basis without BOP involvement. This reform fundamentally shifted the compassionate release process, empowering courts with greater interpretive authority.

2023 Sentencing Guidelines Amendment, U.S. Sentencing Commission

This recent amendment allows courts to consider long sentences exceeding 10 years as a basis for compassionate release if they are now deemed unusually long or unjust. It explicitly permits courts to address disparities between outdated sentences and current sentencing practices.

USSG Amendment 814, U.S. Sentencing Guidelines Manual (2023)

Amendment 814 provides guidelines for compassionate release concerning inmates who were victims of abuse while in custody. It allows inmates with documented experiences of abuse by correctional staff, verified through legal or administrative findings, to request compassionate release under these specific criteria.

APPENDIX D: MOTION TEMPLATE WITH ANNOTATIONS

UNITED STATES DISTRICT COURT
FOR THE
_____ DISTRICT OF _____

[PRISONER'S NAME]
    Petitioner,

v.   [Case No. _____]

UNITED STATES OF AMERICA
    Respondent.

PETITIONER'S PRO SE MOTION FOR COMPASSIONATE RELEASE PURSUANT TO 18 U.S.C. § 3582(c)(1)(A)(i)

I Introduction

[Prisoner's Name], proceeding pro se, respectfully submits this motion for compassionate release pursuant to 18 U.S.C. § 3582(c)(1)(A), requesting that the Court exercise its discretion to reduce their sentence based on extraordinary and compelling circumstances.

APPENDICES

II. Background
   • Conviction and Sentence:

[Prisoner's Name] was convicted of [List Charges] on [Conviction Date] and sentenced to [Length of Sentence] by [Judge's Name]. The case involved [Briefly describe the context of the case, referencing *United States v. Brooker* to highlight the broad interpretation of "extraordinary and compelling reasons."]

III. Grounds for Release
   • A. Medical Condition:

[Prisoner's Name] suffers from [Describe specific medical conditions] that significantly impair their ability to serve their sentence. Medical records (attached) substantiate the severity of these conditions.

   • B. Family Circumstances:

[Prisoner's Name] is seeking release due to [Outline family issues, such as a serious illness in the family or a need for the prisoner's support in critical times.]

   • C. Rehabilitation Efforts:

[Prisoner's Name] has made significant efforts toward rehabilitation by participating in [Detail specific programs or classes, demonstrating a commitment to reform and readiness to reintegrate into society.]

IV. The Impact of Release

[Prisoner's Name] believes that their release would not only benefit their family but also contribute positively to the community. [Include a brief description of reintegration plans and potential support from family and community members.]

V. Conclusion

In light of the extraordinary and compelling reasons presented, [Prisoner's Name] respectfully requests that the Court grant this motion for compassionate release under 18 U.S.C. § 3582(c)(1)(A). The Court's consideration of this request is greatly appreciated.

Date: [Insert Date]

Respectfully submitted,
[Prisoner's Signature]
[Prisoner's Name]
[Prisoner's Prison ID Number]
[Prisoner's Current Address]
[City, State, Zip]

Attachments:
1 Medical Records
2 Letters of Support
3 Documentation of Rehabilitation Efforts

APPENDIX E: FREQUENTLY ASKED QUESTIONS (FAQS)

1. What is compassionate release?

Compassionate release is a legal mechanism that allows federal prisoners to seek a reduction in their sentence under extraordinary and compelling circumstances. This may include serious medical conditions, family emergencies, or other significant hardships that were not considered at the time of sentencing.

2. Who is eligible for compassionate release?

APPENDICES

Eligibility criteria for compassionate release vary but generally include:

- Serving a federal sentence (not applicable to state prisoners).
- Demonstrating extraordinary and compelling reasons, such as terminal illness, debilitating health issues, age-related decline, or being a primary caregiver for a dependent.
- Having served a significant portion of the sentence, typically at least 10 years or more for long sentences.

It's crucial to review the specific guidelines set forth by the Bureau of Prisons (BOP) and recent amendments to the Sentencing Guidelines.

3. How do I file for compassionate release?

The process generally involves several steps:

1. Prepare the Motion: Draft a comprehensive motion detailing your circumstances and supporting documents.
2. Gather Supporting Documents: Collect medical records, letters of support from family or community members, and any relevant legal documents.
3. Submit to the BOP: Present the motion to the warden of the institution where you are housed. If denied, you can appeal to the court.
4. File with the Court: If the BOP does not respond or denies your request, you may file a motion directly with the court.

4. What types of supporting documents should I include?

Supporting documents can include:

- Medical records that substantiate health claims.
- Character reference letters from family, friends, or community members.
- Any documentation that highlights your rehabilitation efforts or positive behavior while incarcerated.
- Records of any extraordinary circumstances impacting your situation.

5. What happens if the government opposes my motion?

If the government files a response in opposition, it is important to reply promptly. Address their arguments directly, especially if they conflict with your BOP records. Provide evidence to refute claims about being a danger to society or any assertions that you are not eligible for release.

6. How long does the compassionate release process take?

The duration of the process can vary significantly based on individual circumstances and the specific BOP institution. It can take several months for a motion to be reviewed, and court timelines may also impact the length of the process.

7. Can I appeal if my motion is denied?

Yes, if your motion for compassionate release is denied, you can appeal the decision. This process will involve filing a notice of appeal in the court that heard your original motion and presenting your case for reconsideration.

8. Where can I find more information about compassionate release?

APPENDICES

You can find more information about compassionate release by consulting the following resources:

- The Bureau of Prisons website: BOP Compassionate Release
- Legal advocacy organizations such as the American Civil Liberties Union (ACLU) or the Sentencing Project.
- Recent legal texts and commentaries on federal sentencing law.

This FAQ section aims to provide clarity on the compassionate release process and help readers navigate their paths to seeking justice. If you have additional questions or require further assistance, consider reaching out to legal professionals specializing in federal law.

APPENDIX F: SAMPLE SUPPORTING DOCUMENTS

Sample Letter from a Family Member
   [Your Name]
   [Your Address]
   [City, State, Zip Code]
   [Email Address]
   [Date]
   [Recipient Name]
   [Title/Position]
   [Institution/Court Name]
   [Address]
   [City, State, Zip Code]
   Dear [Recipient Name],
   I am writing to express my heartfelt support for the

compassionate release of my [relation, e.g., brother, sister, father], [Prisoner's Name], who is currently incarcerated at [Facility Name].

[Prisoner's Name] has been a loving and devoted family member throughout our lives, always prioritizing the well-being of those around him/her. The circumstances of his/her imprisonment have been profoundly challenging for our family, especially given the serious health issues he/she is facing, including [briefly describe health issues].

His/her absence has left a significant void in our family, and I firmly believe that allowing [Prisoner's Name] to return home would not only aid in his/her recovery but also enable him/her to support our family during this critical time.

I respectfully request that you consider this letter as a testament to [Prisoner's Name]'s character and the urgent need for compassionate release based on the exceptional circumstances we are currently facing.

Thank you for considering my request.

Sincerely,

[Your Name]

Sample Letter from a Healthcare Professional

[Healthcare Professional's Name]
[Title/Position]
[Facility/Practice Name]
[Address]
[City, State, Zip Code]
[Email Address]
[Date]
[Recipient Name]
[Title/Position]
[Institution/Court Name]
[Address]

[City, State, Zip Code]
Dear [Recipient Name],

I am writing as [Prisoner's Name]'s healthcare provider at [Facility Name]. I have been overseeing his/her medical care since [date], and I am deeply concerned about his/her current health condition.

[Prisoner's Name] is suffering from [specific medical conditions], which have been exacerbated by the conditions of his/her incarceration. These health issues require ongoing treatment that is not adequately addressed within the prison system.

It is my professional opinion that [Prisoner's Name] would benefit immensely from compassionate release to allow for more effective medical care and to facilitate his/her recovery in a supportive environment.

Thank you for your attention to this matter. I hope you will consider the impact that compassionate release would have on [Prisoner's Name]'s health and well-being.

Sincerely,
[Healthcare Professional's Name]

Sample Letter from a Community Member
[Your Name]
[Your Address]
[City, State, Zip Code]
[Email Address]
[Date]
[Recipient Name]
[Title/Position]
[Institution/Court Name]
[Address]
[City, State, Zip Code]

Dear [Recipient Name],

I am writing to lend my support to [Prisoner's Name], who is seeking compassionate release from [Facility Name]. As a member of [describe your relationship to the prisoner, e.g., local community, church, etc.], I have witnessed firsthand the positive impact that [Prisoner's Name] has had on our community.

His/her commitment to [describe any community service or positive contributions] exemplifies his/her character and potential for rehabilitation. I believe that with the opportunity for compassionate release, [Prisoner's Name] can continue to contribute positively to society and support his/her family.

I respectfully urge you to consider this letter as a reflection of the respect and support [Prisoner's Name] has earned within our community.

Thank you for your time and consideration.

Sincerely,

[Your Name]

These sample letters demonstrate how effective supporting documents can highlight the prisoner's character, health issues, and the impact of their incarceration on family and community. Personal anecdotes, specific examples, and emotional appeals can enhance the strength of these letters in the compassionate release process.

APPENDIX G: GLOSSARY OF LEGAL TERMS

1. Compassionate Release

A legal mechanism that allows incarcerated individuals to have their sentences reduced or modified due to extraordinary and compelling circumstances, such as serious medical conditions or family emergencies. This process can provide an avenue for those who are suffering or who present a low risk to society to reenter the community.

2. Extraordinary and Compelling Reasons

A standard established by the U.S. Sentencing Guidelines to determine eligibility for compassionate release. Factors may include terminal illnesses, debilitating medical conditions, age-related issues, or significant changes in family circumstances.

3. Motion for Compassionate Release

A formal request submitted to a court seeking a reduction in sentence based on compassionate grounds. The motion must outline the reasons for the request and provide supporting documentation.

4. United States Sentencing Guidelines (USSG)

A set of rules established to create a uniform policy for sentencing in federal criminal cases. The guidelines provide a framework for judges to determine appropriate sentences based on the severity of the offense and the offender's criminal history.

5. Bureau of Prisons (BOP)

The federal agency responsible for managing and regulating federal prisons and the prisoners housed within them. The BOP also plays a role in the compassionate release process by reviewing requests and making recommendations to the courts.

6. Precedent

A legal principle or rule established in a previous case that is binding or persuasive in subsequent cases. Precedents can significantly influence the outcomes of motions for compassionate release, particularly those established by higher courts.

7. Judicial Discretion

The authority granted to judges to make decisions based on their judgment and interpretation of the law. In compassionate release cases, judges have discretion to consider the individual circumstances of the prisoner and the merits of the motion.

8. Opposition

A formal response filed by the government or prosecution against a motion, contesting the claims made by the prisoner and arguing against the grant of compassionate release.

9. Hearing

A legal proceeding before a judge or court where evidence is presented, and arguments are made regarding the motion for compassionate release. A hearing may involve testimony from the prisoner, family members, or experts.

10. Sentencing Disparities

Differences in sentencing outcomes among similar cases or individuals based on factors such as race, socio-economic status, or the judge's discretion. Addressing these disparities is a key aspect of discussions around compassionate release and fairness in the justice system.

11. Recidivism

The tendency of a convicted criminal to reoffend or relapse into criminal behavior after serving a sentence. Evaluating the risk of recidivism is crucial in determining eligibility for compassionate release.

12. First Step Act

A landmark piece of legislation passed in 2018 aimed at reforming the federal prison system and reducing recidivism. It expanded eligibility for compassionate release and modified sentencing laws to promote fairer treatment.

13. Pro Se

A Latin term meaning "on one's own behalf." In legal

contexts, it refers to individuals who represent themselves in court without the assistance of an attorney.

14. Affidavit

A written statement made under oath, used as evidence in court. Affidavits may be submitted in support of a motion for compassionate release to provide testimony regarding the prisoner's character or health condition.

15. Collateral Consequences

Legal penalties or disabilities that are imposed on individuals after their criminal convictions, which may affect their ability to reintegrate into society even after serving their time.

16. Cumulative Argument

A legal strategy that involves presenting multiple pieces of evidence or reasoning that collectively strengthen the case for compassionate release. Rather than relying on a single compelling reason, a cumulative argument showcases a range of factors—such as the prisoner's character, rehabilitation efforts, health issues, and family support—that together create a persuasive case for reducing the sentence. This approach emphasizes the holistic view of the prisoner's situation, illustrating that various circumstances, when combined, warrant a reconsideration of the sentence.

This glossary serves as a helpful reference for understanding the legal terms and jargon often encountered in the compassionate release process, making it more accessible for readers who may not have a legal background.

APPENDIX H: TIMELINE OF KEY LEGISLATIVE CHANGES

1984: Comprehensive Crime Control Act

- Overview: This act established the U.S. Sentencing Commission and introduced federal sentencing guidelines, significantly impacting how sentences were determined.
- Impact: It made it more challenging for prisoners to receive early release by imposing strict guidelines on sentencing.

1994: Violent Crime Control and Law Enforcement Act

- Overview: Included provisions that aimed to reduce crime through tougher penalties and extended sentences for certain offenses.
- Impact: Contributed to an increase in incarceration rates, further limiting options for compassionate release.

2007: First Step Act

- Overview: While this act primarily focused on reducing recidivism and enhancing prison programs, it also modified the compassionate release process.
- Impact: Allowed prisoners to file motions for compassionate release directly to the courts, instead of through the Bureau of Prisons (BOP) only.

2018: First Step Act of 2018

- Overview: This comprehensive reform legislation

aimed at improving conditions for inmates and reducing sentences for non-violent offenders.
- Impact: Expanded eligibility for compassionate release by providing clearer guidelines for determining "extraordinary and compelling reasons" for release and allowing prisoners to seek release after serving 10 years.

2020: United States v. Brooker (also known as United States v. Zullo (2d Cir. 2020)

- Overview: A landmark ruling by the Second Circuit Court of Appeals that clarified the standard for compassionate release.
- Impact: Established that district courts have the authority to determine what constitutes "extraordinary and compelling reasons," setting a precedent that influenced subsequent cases and interpretations of compassionate release criteria.

2021: USSG Amendment 814

- Overview: An amendment to the U.S. Sentencing Guidelines that refined the definition of "extraordinary and compelling reasons" for compassionate release.
- Impact: Specifically addressed cases involving sexual or physical abuse of prisoners, making it easier for those affected to apply for compassionate release.

2022: Continued Legislative Discussions

- Overview: Ongoing discussions in Congress regarding criminal justice reform and the potential expansion of compassionate release eligibility.
- Impact: Reflects the growing recognition of the need for reform in the federal criminal justice system, although no significant new laws have yet been passed.

This timeline highlights the crucial milestones in the evolution of compassionate release laws and the legal framework surrounding them, illustrating the shifting landscape towards a more compassionate and just system.

APPENDIX I: CONTACT INFORMATION FOR ADVOCACY GROUPS

This appendix provides a list of organizations that offer support for individuals seeking compassionate release or advocating for criminal justice reform. These groups can provide resources, guidance, and advocacy to help navigate the compassionate release process.

1. Families Against Mandatory Minimums (FAMM)

- Description: FAMM is dedicated to reforming mandatory sentencing laws and advocating for fair sentencing practices.
- Website: www.famm.org
- Phone: 202-822-6700

2. The Sentencing Project

APPENDICES

- Description: This organization conducts research and advocates for reforms in the criminal justice system, focusing on reducing incarceration rates and promoting fair sentencing.
- Website: www.sentencingproject.org
- Phone: 202-628-0871

3. American Civil Liberties Union (ACLU)

- Description: The ACLU works to protect civil liberties, including the rights of prisoners and the fight against mass incarceration.
- Website: www.aclu.org
- Phone: 212-549-2500

4. The Innocence Project

- Description: Focused on wrongful convictions, this organization also provides guidance on various post-conviction remedies, including compassionate release.
- Website: www.innocenceproject.org
- Phone: 212-364-5340

5. Prison Fellowship

- Description: This Christian organization advocates for restorative justice and provides support for prisoners and their families, including assistance with compassionate release applications.
- Website: www.prisonfellowship.org
- Phone: 703-481-0000

6. Justice Policy Institute

- Description: A research and policy organization that advocates for reforms in the justice system to improve outcomes for prisoners and their communities.
- Website: www.justicepolicy.org
- Phone: 202-558-7974

7. ACLU National Prison Project

- Description: This project works to protect the rights of prisoners and advocates for reform to improve conditions of confinement.
- Website: www.aclu.org/issues/prisoners-rights
- Phone: 202-549-2500

8. Human Rights Watch

- Description: This organization conducts research and advocacy on human rights issues, including conditions of confinement and the treatment of prisoners.
- Website: www.hrw.org
- Phone: 212-290-4700